Hitler's SS

Richard Grunberger

Hitler's SS

DORSET PRESS/NEW YORK

This edition published by Dorset Press,
a division of Barnes & Noble, Inc.,
by arrangement with Weidenfeld & Nicholson, Ltd.

1993 Dorset Press

ISBN 1-56619-152-1

Printed and bound in the United States of America

M 9 8 7 6 5 4 3

To I.G. (1883–1934)

Contents

Acknowledgements

The author and publishers would like to thank the people and institutions below for permission to reproduce the photographs on the pages mentioned after their names.

Archiv Gerstenberg, 17 (bottom), 18 (top), 73 (top), 74 (bottom), 75 (bottom), 90 (bottom), 92, 109; Comité International d'Auschwitz, 90 (top); Bavaria Verlag, 89 (top and bottom); Historical Research Unit, 20 (top), 38 (top), 57 (top and bottom), 58 (top and bottom right), 60 (top), 61, 64 (bottom right), 91; Novosti Press, 78 (top and bottom); Popperfoto, 38 110 (top); Sudverlag, 20 (bottom), 37 (bottom), 59, 60 (bottom), 63 (top and bottom), 73 (top), 80 (top); Ullstein, 17 (top), 18 (bottom), 37 (top) 38 (bottom), 40, 62, 64 (top), 74 (top), 79 (top), 80 (top), 110 (bottom), 111 (top), 112; Radio Times Hulton Picture Library, 10.

1

From Beer Cellars
to Power

ELEVENTH DAY OF THE ELEVENTH MONTH OF 1918: WHILE THE
Great War expired all over Europe in Germany the Weimar Republic
struggled towards birth. Amid revolutionary alarums and excursions
German democracy – a slack balloon filling out in an airless jar – expanded
to fill the vacuum created by the Kaiser and his generals absconding
into exile (or retirement) one step ahead of unavoidable military defeat.

In the aftermath of a collapse so total and unexpected that it soon
made many Germans say (with Field Marshal Hindenburg), 'We were
not beaten in battle but stabbed in the back by traitors', the Republic's
first Parliament met at Weimar to set up responsible government,
introduce universal suffrage and establish civilian control over the
Reichswehr, the hundred-thousand-man army permitted by the
Versailles Treaty of 1919.

But the radical elements behind the strikes and mutinies that had
accompanied military defeat judged piecemeal political reform an in-
sufficient substitute for fundamental economic change and attempted –
in Berlin, Bavaria and elsewhere – to transform postwar readjustment
into social revolution.

Although in Berlin the Spartacists (forerunners of the German
Communist Party) failed quickly and bloodily, a Soviet-style regime
assumed power in Bavaria. It had a programme of workers' control,
land reform and popular participation in government. However, it was
soon crushed by a combined force of armed right-wing gangs derived
from Reichswehr and Freikorps irregulars.

It was here at Munich, savagely purged of Red Revolution, that the
story of the SS began. Heinrich Himmler (born in Munich in 1900),
bespectacled, narrow-chested, a soldier *manqué*, had, to his chagrin,
missed action in war, but had belonged briefly to one of the Freikorps
that 'liberated' the Bavarian capital. Adolf Hitler, too, found himself at
Munich in 1919 awaiting demobilization.

Before discharge he attended one of the soldiers' indoctrination
classes with which the Reichswehr officer corps supplemented its armed

combat of left-wing subversion. Hitler attracted the favourable attention of his instructors and was ordered to infiltrate, for counter-revolutionary ends, the suspiciously named National Socialist German Workers' Party – in reality no more than a conventicle of beer-parlour politicians.

By January 1920 Hitler, now a civilian, had made himself leader of the National Socialists and began to establish a reputation (and following) throughout Munich by his tirades against the 'Jew-ridden' Weimar Republic which he delivered before steadily increasing audiences of disoriented petty-bourgeois citizens.

At Nazi meetings the fury of Hitler's words fused with the activity of squads of strong-arm men to generate a noticeable aura of violence. Before one particular meeting in late 1921 Hitler informed his stewards: 'None of us will leave this hall unless we are carried out as corpses. If any coward shrinks back I will personally rip off his arm-band and cap-badge.'

Early on, a military bodyguard had been provided for him by Captain Röhm (a corpulent Reichswehr officer with contacts among the top brass), and this unit, soon reconstituted as the Party's private strong-arm squad, formed the original nucleus of the SS. Its leader was a stationery salesman, Josef Berchtold; Hitler's three initial personal bodyguards were Ulrich Graf, Emil Maurice and Christian Weber – the first a butcher and amateur wrestler, the second a watchmaker turned chauffeur, and the third a bloodstock-dealer who doubled as a beer-cellar bouncer.

By November 1923 when the Nazis made their first – and short-lived – impact on German postwar history, the so-called 'Stosstrupp Hitler' numbered fifty members, but in fact constituted no more than a special sub-unit of the *Sturmabteilungen* (SA, or storm-troops) – the two thousand-strong private army Röhm had built up for the Party since his discharge from the Reichswehr.

The abortive beer-cellar putsch in Munich on 9 November 1923 cost about a dozen fatal *Stosstrupp* or SA casualties and resulted in the short-term imprisonment of Hitler, as well as the temporary proscription of his party. Released in December 1924, Hitler reconstituted the Party, and in the following April set up a new 'staff guard', subsequently renamed *Schutzstaffeln*, or SS for short. Himmler, who since participating in the Munich Putsch had worked for the Party in various ways, as secretary to the Nazi Reichstag deputy Gregor Strasser, as a roving speaker, and as surveyor of secret arms dumps, now joined the SS and received membership number 168. In the following year, at the Party's annual para-military jamboree at Weimar (forerunner of the mammoth Nuremberg Rallies of the 1930s) the SS marched past Hitler, who awarded them the 'bloodflag' – allegedly stained with the gore of the Munich Putsch casualties – for services rendered on that heroic occasion. (The *Stosstrupp*'s actual exploit on the 'Day of National Uprising' had consisted of wrecking the Munich Social Democrat newspaper's printing presses; paradoxically the SS's primary non-combatant duties now also revolved around journalism: they were sent out to collect subscriptions and canvass advertisements for the Party-owned newspaper *Der Völkische Beobachter*.)

At the Weimar Rally Himmler had already acted as deputy leader of the SS, and in January 1929 Hitler appointed him Reichsführer SS. The twenty-nine-year-old 'eternal subaltern' had thus achieved the very height of ambition; but his new, grandiloquent title obscured the fact that the Munich-based SS headquarters only controlled three hundred men (the Berlin SS continued independently under Kurt Daluege, Goebbels' chief bully-boy) and that moreover the SS as such formed a mere sub-section of Röhm's much larger SA.

Yet at the same time, despite its theoretically subordinate position and small size, the black-uniformed SS could be said to outrank Röhm's brownshirts in the way a Roman Emperor's Praetorian Guard outranked the Roman legions. SA implied marching with the big battalions, SS meant membership of a select élite.

In Party parlance 'select' connoted hand-picked as well as thoroughbred – and since race formed the key dogma of the Nazi creed it was hardly surprising that some of its high priests had served apprenticeships in animal husbandry. The Nazi agricultural leader Walther Darré, who aimed at transforming Germany's farmers into a 'new nobility of blood and soil', was once a pig-breeder, while Himmler (a keen disciple of Darré's human bloodstock theories) had been engaged in chicken-farming outside Munich at the time of his appointment to the leadership of the SS.

Given the Nazi mystique of the soil, Himmler's earlier choice of a career would appear to have been quite apt, although it in fact represented something of a step down from his social background. His father, *Studienrat* (literally 'Study Counsellor') Gebhard Himmler, had in turn tutored one of Bavaria's royal princes (Heinrich of Wittelsbach, godfather to the SS leader), taught at a Munich grammar school and been headmaster of a provincial one. In other words, the sometime chicken-farmer had been born into the *Bildungsbürgertum* (the educated bourgeoisie), an esteemed, though not over-affluent, status group within Wilhelmine society.

The Himmlers' family life seems to have been close and harmonious, with the mother dutifully carrying out her prescribed role of *Hausfrau* and the *Herr Studienrat* self-importantly inculcating respect for the national past and established authority in his compliant children. In the 1920s occurred an episode highly revealing of the family ethos and young Himmler's cast of mind: on hearing that his elder brother Gebhard had become engaged, Heinrich commissioned a detective agency to investigate the fiancée's past, and when circumstantial evidence pointed to an earlier liaison, he prevailed upon Gebhard to break off the engagement.

At this time the twenty-four-year-old puritan was himself still a virgin. As far as his more conventional education was concerned, he had matriculated from his father's school and gone on to complete a three-year diploma course in agriculture at Munich University. At the university Himmler belonged to a duelling fraternity (wearing his rim-less pince-nez even when duelling), did unpaid clerical jobs for the students' committee, kept a diary, attended Mass on Sundays and worked at self-improvement in two directions: to achieve great mascu-linity he practised shooting and subjected his unprepossessing body to athletic exercises, while in order to acquire greater social facility, he took dancing lessons and sought (platonic) contact with the opposite sex. Although immersion in political activity subsequently helped him to realize these aims to some extent, Himmler, the desk-bound pro-genitor of 'blond beasts', was never – not even at the height of his career – entirely to overcome his sense of social and physical inadequacy.

In 1928 he married Margarete Concerzowo, who was seven years his senior and owned a small nursing-home in Berlin, to which city Party business had taken him a year earlier. Though Marga Himmler had no strong political beliefs her nursing background led her to share Heinrich's interests in the pseudo-scientific folklore of homeopathy and herbal cures. The couple also shared a less esoteric interest in the economic viability of a smallholding they had bought with Marga's money at Waltrudering (ten miles from Munich) and on which they kept fifty hens. This joint absorption, however, did not long outlive the birth of Gudrun Himmler in 1929, after which the farm and the child became Marga's means of dealing with the life of a grass widow to which she was progressively reduced by Heinrich's other preoccupations – political as well as emotional. The year of Gudrun's birth saw the world lose its fragile postwar equilibrium in the wake of the Wall Street Crash. While share values plunged crazily, the Nazis' political stock rose fast – at an even faster rate than Germany's unemployment figures. The September 1930 elections made the twelve-man Nazi *Fraktion* in the Reichstag mushroom into an ominous contingent of a hundred and seven that was to help nullify all attempts at parliamentary government.

SS membership began to reach four and eventually five figures during 1931, a year in which the 'Order of the Death's Head' (so-called after the insignia on the SS men's peaked caps) took on ever more distinctive features. The blood-and-soil ideologue Darré set up the SS Race and Settlement Office (*Rasse-und Siedlungs-Hauptamt*, or RUSHA) which combined eugenic marriage-broking with researches into foreign Aryan stock potentially capable of 'Germanization' at a future date.

One of the Race and Settlement Office's first innovations was the SS marriage code under which official approbation of an SS man's marriage was made dependent on proof of the bride's Aryan descent – as far back as 1750 – and on her character, sanity, physical health and potential child-bearing capacity. RUSHA also kept stud records of the entire SS, and every individual member was issued with a *Sippenbuch* (clan book) containing the marriage code, in which the eugenic statistics of his wife and progeny had to be entered.

It was in 1931, too, that the Order of the Death's Head recruited the man who, more than any other, was to lend a chilling authenticity to that title: Reinhard Heydrich. Tall and fair, self-assured and intelligent, athletic and artistically gifted, Heydrich was in many ways the antithesis of the Reichsführer, whose deputy he soon became. The son of an opera singer turned music teacher, Heydrich started to train as a violinist, became caught up in the Freikorps movement at sixteen, and subsequently joined the Navy, in which he rose to the position of Signals Officer attached to Intelligence. Despite his Freikorps background his decision to join the SS in 1931 had not been politically motivated; it was in fact the rather indirect by-product of the sort of sexual peccadillo to which he remained addicted until his death.

A little earlier two strands of Heydrich's sex life had become awkwardly entangled: his engagement to the headstrong Lina von Osten had caused the father of Lina's more compliant predecessor to request that the *Herr Leutnant* make an honest woman of his daughter. On receipt of the classic reply 'No self-respecting officer could marry a girl who had given herself to him so readily', the father (who had influence with Heydrich's superior, Admiral Raeder) satisfied family honour by instigating the philanderer's dismissal from the service.

It was Lina von Osten, a dedicated Nazi, who advised her future husband to apply for a post in the expanding SS organization. The new recruit's personality and Naval Intelligence background impressed Himmler sufficiently to appoint Heydrich head of the newly created *Sicherheitsdienst* (SD for short), the intra-Party espionage service set up after the Stennes Affair when Kurt Daluege, the Berlin SS commander, had been hard put to crush an anti-Hitler rebellion among the capital's stormtroopers.

Daluege's action had earned a commendation from Hitler culminating in the phrase 'SS man, your honour is loyalty!', and in an amended form this became the motto of the Death's Head Order: hereafter SS belt buckles proclaimed *Unsere Ehre heisst Treue* – our honour is named loyalty – in (godless) imitation of the 'Gott mit uns' legend engraved on army belt buckles under the Kaiser.

Also in 1931 Himmler was appointed as head of security at the *Braune Haus*, the newly acquired Party headquarters in Munich. The following year saw a further decline in the country's economic and political stability while the Nazi electoral advance assumed landslide proportions. By April 1932 SS strength stood at thirty thousand and the stormtroops disposed of ten times that number. The new brownshirt contingents were often unemployed, eager for soup-kitchen handouts, free uniforms and *camaraderie*; while the élitist SS attracted professional men, academics, ex-officers, and even such sprigs of the nobility as Prince Waldeck-Pyrmont and the Prince of Mecklenburg.

The flood tide of recruitment occurred during the opening months of 1933. On 30 January Hitler was appointed Chancellor and at a general election five weeks later – the last to be held in Germany during the Nazi era – he won a narrow majority which became a mandate to destroy democracy. The seizure of power inspired such a rich crop of Nazi recruits (derisively known as 'March violets') that in May the Party froze membership at the current level. With direct entry temporarily denied to them, thousands of young – and not-so-young –

The Munich *putsch* of 9 November 1923. Steel-helmeted storm troopers arrest city councillors

Storm troopers at machine-gun practice outside Munich (1923)

A Nazi orator addressing a crowd in the centre of Munich on 9 November 1923

Himmler as a standard bearer during the Munich *putsch*

On the road to power: Hitler and some top Nazis in 1932. Next to Himmler (front left) stands Frick; Goebbels is left behind Hitler and Goering on the far right

Hitler flanked by SS body-guards (left to right: Schaub, Schreck, Maurer, Schneider) in 1925. Julius Schaub subsequently became his adjutant, and Julius Schreck his chauffeur. Notice the half erased figure of a fifth body-guard

Ulrich Graf who had been wounded protecting Hitler on 9 November 1923 hopefuls streamed into the Party's auxiliary formations (the SA, SS, motorized NSKK), to be ahead of the field when the moratorium came to an end.

Reasserting the principle of selectivity at the heart of the SS ethos, Himmler, early in 1934, ordered that fifty thousand black-uniformed March violets be weeded out. This domestic clean-out, however, was an innocent interlude alongside the cannibalistic rite of purification the SS performed among German society at large and (after 1939) throughout most of Europe.

Two German terms, soon to enter every civilized language, became shorthand for this purification: KZ (short for *Konzentrationslager*, or concentration camp) and Gestapo (short for *Geheime Staatspolizei* or secret state police).

The seizure of power was accompanied by the rounding up, maltreatment and torture (often ending in death) of thousands of anti-Nazis. Arrested by the Gestapo, or police 'auxiliaries', these prisoners, for whom the existing police jails proved inadequate, were lodged in concentration camps. In 1933 neither the Gestapo nor the concentration camps were the streamlined institutions they subsequently became and their control was disputed between Nazi administrators, the SA and the SS. Local Gauleiters and SA leaders set up so-called 'wild' concentration camps, and on occasion – as at Papenburg camp near Osnabruck – rival agencies of the Nazi regime fought virtual pitched battles in disputes over the running of camps.

In March 1933 Himmler became Police President of Munich, with Heydrich as his assistant; June saw the creation of Dachau concentration camp – model for all subsequent Nazi hells on earth.

Camp routine, enforced by SS and SA men, whose only *alma mater* had been the drill-hall, was a sadistic perversion of military training. KZ inmates had to answer roll-calls, salute, stand to attention, report themselves present, and proceed at the double – and to endure the vilest forms of barrack-square abuse in the process. For breach of regulations they were liable, according to the official disciplinary code, to undergo any of the following: punitive labour, punitive drill, extended roll-calls, confiscation of mail, reduction of rations, solitary confinement, confinement in the dark, incarceration in a stand-up cell, twenty-five strokes on the posterior (covered or bare), suspension from a pole by the wrists, transfer to a punishment battalion, death by shooting or by hanging.

The first commandant of Dachau was Theodor Eicke, whom

Death's Head – symbol of the SS which was to become an emblem of terror throughout Germany and Europe.

Himmler had a little earlier sprung from Würzburg psychiatric clinic, to which Gauleiter Bürckel had consigned him – in a strait-jacket – as a lunatic constituting a public danger. Eicke, the son of a railway clerk, had seen war service in the Pay Corps and had subsequently joined the police, but failed to gain promotion. By contrast he managed to carve out a remarkable career in the SS, advancing within little over a year from command of the Third Reich's seminal KZ to control of the entire concentration-camp system, which in autumn 1934 comprised eight major institutions, ranging from Dachau to the dreaded Kolumbia Haus in Berlin.

The guards at Dachau – enrolled in the so-called Death's Head units – were largely drawn from the lowest stratum of Bavarian society: moronic and brutalized peasant types who in a period of reviving employment looked to SS service as a socially acceptable (not to say prestigious) means of avoiding honest labour. Irascibly primitive, these Dachau guards nursed a particular animus against intellectuals and Jews (two partly overlapping categories), and prisoners with academic titles or an offensively scholarly mien – such as wearers of spectacles – elicited even more vicious reactions from them than others. The camp personnel's native coarseness – thus the camp clerk's enquiry about the name of an inmate's mother might be phrased as 'Which Jew-whore shitted you out?' – was intensified by conditioning: during training, members of the Death's Head units would alternate three weeks of gruelling military drill with one week's concentration-camp guard duty, in the course of which they had to watch whippings and hangings alongside the prisoners.

As far as the outside world went, the SS arranged things so that the German public's knowledge about concentration camps was simultaneously – and paradoxically – both widespread and patchy. Though all Germans were vaguely aware of their existence, concentration camps remained taboo topics surrounded by secrecy and dread. But since total secrecy would have detracted from the value of the camps as deterrents, a minimal supply of information about what went on behind those electrified barbed-wire entanglements, searchlights and machine-gun towers was allowed to reach the outside world. Thus the stereotyped formula 'shot while trying to escape', behind which official announcements (on the inside pages of newspapers and in communications to next-of-kin) camouflaged the premeditated murder of camp inmates, soon passed into common usage as a universally understood cynical euphemism.

As time went on the unofficial grapevine which supplemented the official media as an essential source of information also spread knowledge of the SS practice whereby the next-of-kin of murdered prisoners would be informed of their bereavement by the postal delivery of an urn containing the deceased's ashes.

Even so, many citizens of the Third Reich remained fully persuaded that concentration camps subserved the professed Nazi aim – enshrined in the inscription *'Arbeit macht frei'* ('Work makes you free') above the camp gates at Dachau – of re-educating and salvaging prisoners for the German *Volksgemeinschaft* (folk community) through the educative agencies of hard work and discipline.

In tenuous corroboration of this myth, 'work-shy elements' – which in official Nazi terminology meant workers who had twice rejected employment offered them without good reason – would be consigned by the Gestapo to Dachau and similar institutions; but the 'work-shy' were in fact only one among many groups in the concentration-camp population.

The diversity of the camp inmates stemmed from Heydrich's and Himmler's adaptation of the Roman *'Divide et Impera'* to the conditions of their own slave state-within-a-state. The 'work-shy' belonged to the concentration-camp category *Asoziale*, alongside beggars, vagabonds, gypsies, prostitutes, alcoholics, brawlers, psychopaths, imbeciles and profiteers. These were intermingled with members of such other categories as professional and congenital criminals, homosexuals, Jehovah's Witnesses, anti-Nazis (ranging from Communists to Christians) and finally Jews.

To prevent stirrings of solidarity among these disparate groups, the SS furthermore created an internal camp hierarchy – such us block elders, or hut leaders – of congenital criminals whose power over their unfortunate subordinates, of whatever category, was almost as total and arbitrary as that of the guards. (KZ personnel exercised such unlimited dominion over the life and death of their shaven-headed, zebra-stripe-garbed prisoners that the Socialist poet Erich Mühsam, for instance, obediently hanged himself upon the expiry of a three-day time-limit the commandant of Sachsenhausen had set him.)

And yet these lords over life and death were themselves subject to the chill control and scrutiny of the Gestapo-staffed 'Political Departments' that functioned within the administration of each concentration camp as part of the command structure built up by Heydrich. The Gestapo itself had evolved according to Darwinian laws out of a tangle of warring institutions – old and new – whose vicious in-fighting continued for months after the seizure of power. Its relatively innocuous antecedents were the political police departments that had previously functioned in Weimar Germany's various constituent states – Prussia, Bavaria, Saxony, and the rest.

The Gestapo's founding father was not Himmler – who was merely police chief of Bavaria in Spring 1933 – but Hermann Göring, who as Prime Minister of Prussia 'seconded' SA and SS killer squads to the Prussian political police during the reign of terror that followed the burning of the Reichstag (27 February 1933). This initial staffing of the new force by rival cliques turned its Prinz Albrechtstrasse headquarters into a small-scale battleground. Colleagues tried to arrest each other and alerted friends by phone before going to the toilet – in case they failed to return. Artur Nebe, head of the Criminal Police and a fast-rising member of the SS hierarchy, would slip the safety-catch of his revolver as he entered the building through the back door and would hug the walls as he climbed the staircase.

But these were no more than teething troubles, which in no way diminished the Gestapo's effectiveness as an instrument of totalitarian terror. Himmler and Heydrich, who during the interim had fused all the existing political police forces into one, took complete charge of this instrument in April 1934 and subsequently made it steadily more efficient by applying German thoroughness and ingenuity to techniques as old as Torquemada's or as contemporary as those of the OGPU.

The Germans and (after 1939) non-Germans who passed through the cellars of the Gestapo faced torture by a variety of means: flaying with cow-hide whips; alternate drowning in bathtubs filled with cold water and resuscitation; electric shocks through wires attached to feet, hands, ears, penis and anus; the smashing of testicles in a special press; hanging with wrists manacled behind one's back; the infliction of burns with matches or a soldering iron. (A particular refinement consisted of torturing a woman within a prisoner's hearing and informing him that she was his wife.)

The institution equipped with this sort of expertise was finally, under legislation passed in February 1936, given retroactive legal status and simultaneously placed above the law. (Since 1933 the only formality required to despatch a German citizen to a concentration camp had consisted of a Gestapo official's insertion of his name on the appropriate form.) Paragraph 7 of the February 1936 law stated that no appeals were possible against Gestapo directives and that courts were debarred from setting them aside or revising them. In October 1938 Hitler articulated the Nazi concept of legality: 'All means, even if they are not in conformity with existing laws and precedents, are legal if they subserve the will of the Führer.'

Illegal law is the equivalent of organized chaos, but the SS rose above such contradictions by synthesizing them. To Himmler the killers of his Death's Head units were also sperm-donors for a higher form of life; in the Third Reich reality and illusion soon became so inextricably enmeshed that non-Nazis – and even Jews – looked to the SS as a disciplined and therefore relatively reassuring counterweight to Röhm's dissolute stormtroop rowdies.

During the one major internal crisis the Nazi regime was ever to experience – in June 1934 – these two wings of the Party army, respectively black- and brown-uniformed, met in far from open combat; after this purge which later came to be known as 'the Night of the Long Knives' the SA declined into a stage army whilst the SS moved forward to challenge the primacy of the Reichswehr (subsequently the Wehrmacht) as 'sole arms-bearer of the German nation'.

2
Knights of the Long Knives

TO UNDERSTAND THE PHILOSOPHY OF NAZISM ONE HAS TO appreciate that for all its pretensions to the status of an all-embracing ideology it boiled down to one single uncomplicated, though emotionally compelling idea: race-war to the death between German and Jew. This lack of an ideology or even a 'binding' programme left a gap which the regime filled with cynical exercises in opportunism: women, whose place – according to Hitler – was in the home, were forced into factories; the land (eulogized as the unsullied source of German folkdom) was slowly depopulated; and Russia was transformed overnight from arch-enemy to treaty-partner and back again.

Hitler showed comparable opportunism in his relations with the Reichswehr – the single semi-autonomous power that survived in Germany after February 1933. Though this takeover had been accomplished with totalitarian weapons of terror and *Gleichschaltung* (compulsory co-ordination), it was only after the death of the Reich President Hindenburg, who had enjoyed the support of the army, in August 1934 that Hitler's control of the state became complete – and even then it still needed the removal of War Minister von Blomberg and Chief of Staff Fritsch early in 1938 to make the subservience of the military as total as everyone else's.

Hitler's ascendancy over the Party had by contrast been total all along. It was based on personal charisma, the elimination of such potential rivals as the 'leftish' Gregor Strasser, and Olympian remoteness from the battle (for precedence, power and the spoils of office) which was fought in the wings by Ministers, Gauleiters, the Party's political organization, the German Labour Front, the Reich Food Estate, the SS and the SA.

The SA were the self-styled 'People's Army of Nazism' which meant that their strength lay in quantity of numbers rather than quality. However, their leaders, who were frequently ex-officers, were steeped in a military/mercenary ethos and saw themselves as cadres of

Germany's future fighting force. SA commander Röhm actually
aimed to absorb the hundred-thousand-strong Reichswehr in his in-
flated Party army and entertained notions of himself as moulder of a
new fighting machine freed from the trammels of caste and convention
that had hamstrung the German armies in the Great War.

He therefore demonstrated – as well as improved – the effectiveness
of his brownshirt battalions by exercises, manœuvres and the stock-
piling of arms throughout the months following the seizure of power;
and in December 1933 he prevailed upon Hitler to appoint him to the
Reich Cabinet as Minister without Portfolio. Hitler valued Röhm as
the Carnot of the Nazi revolution's *levée en masse* and as an invaluable
contact-man with key military personalities (such as Ludendorff). Since
their early postwar days at Munich the two men had in fact been on
intimate 'Du' terms, whereas Hitler kept himself apart from all his
other paladins by the formal 'Sie'. No secret of the Nazi 'court' had
been as widely disseminated both before and after the seizure of power
as Röhm's homosexual tastes – and yet despite adverse publicity and
internal mutterings Hitler had persistently refused to 'conduct an
inquisition' into the SA chief's (and quite a few of his sub-chiefs')
deviant practices.

As any change in the Nazi pecking-order immediately threw all rival
holders of fiefs into a state of injured rage, Röhm's elevation to Cabinet
rank made Göring and Himmler – after months of vicious in-fighting
for control of the Gestapo – swallow their differences and form an anti-
SA alliance. As Prussian Prime Minister and Reich Air Minister,
Göring was in close touch with the civil service and the armed forces
and shared their common hostility to Röhm's 'revolutionary' schemes,
whilst the SS – who incidentally entertained military ambitions of their
own – could not but be alarmed by the expansionist plans of their
closest rivals.

In February 1934 Röhm took the offensive by submitting a memorandum on military 'reform' to the Reichswehr chiefs – whereupon von
Blomberg pressed Hitler to intervene in the threatening dispute.
The latter imposed a fragile truce on terms under which the SA were
given control over the pre-military and post-service training of army
recruits.

This division of military labour produced understandable disgruntle-
ment among the stormtroops' ranks. At a subsequent SA leaders'
banquet, tongues loosened by alcohol gave utterance to wild if vague
threats against the Führer. However to one Hitler-besotted regional

SA leader, Lutze of Hanover, these flushed outbursts sounded like evidence of treason, and he alerted Hess (Hitler's deputy), von Blomberg and Heydrich. Armed with Lutze's revelations, Heydrich persuaded Himmler of the necessity for an all-out pre-emptive strike against Röhm; and Friedrich Krüger, an ex-SS man in charge of SA training, was deputed to collect incriminating material from within the enemy camp.

While Heydrich was laying his plans with unerring clandestine precision, Röhm pressed the SA's cause in the full glare of publicity, voicing demands for a 'Second Revolution' – which alarmed the bourgeoisie – and enlarging the scope of SA manœuvres to that of army field exercises.

The anti-Röhm front stepped up its preparations in turn; the Reichswehr transferred heavy arms from its arsenals to the SS, and Dachau commandant Eicke's Death's Head units undertook war games with live ammunition. Heydrich, resident in Berlin (like Himmler) since the SS's assumption of full control over the Gestapo in April, spent May compiling a central 'death list'. Regional SS chiefs were asked for names of their own SA rivals, and it was while waiting for these addenda that Heydrich hit on the idea of broadening the projected SA purge into an all-purpose liquidation of key anti-Nazi personages, irrespective of affiliation.

On 17 June von Papen, the Conservative ex-Chancellor who had joined the Hitler cabinet to give it balance, spoke out against Röhm's revolutionary alarums and demanded 'normalization'; this appeal stirred a sufficiently widespread echo to make Hitler suspect a right-wing threat to his regime in addition to the one Röhm posed from the Left. He therefore determined to strike out simultaneously in both directions, albeit – since the Army's goodwill was essential until he finally took over from the near-moribund Hindenburg – under the guise of an alliance with the Conservatives.

After an emergency meeting with Hindenburg and von Blomberg – underscored by Heydrich's dissemination of faked SA plans for a coup – Hitler convoked a conference for 30 June at a Bavarian resort 'to resolve differences' with the SA leadership. Two companies of the crack *Leibstandarte* (Hitler's SS bodyguard) were despatched to Bavaria under their commander Sepp Dietrich, and during the early hours of the projected 'conference' day the assembled SA leaders were dragged from their beds – which some, incidentally, were sharing with male companions – and arrested on charges of high treason. Sepp Dietrich

and Eicke supervised the subsequent executions at Munich's Stadelheim Prison; when the dying Röhm mumbled 'Oh my Führer', Eicke
replied cynically, 'You should have thought of that before!'
From the early morning of 30 June motorized SS units roared
through the streets of Berlin and liquidated – in conformity with
Heydrich's directives for an all-purpose purge – the capital's upper SA
echelons, together with Gregor Strasser, ex-Chancellor Schleicher, the
Catholic leader Dr Klausener, von Papen's press secretary, and many
others. Whilst the latter batch of victims were murdered in their
homes, many SA executions took place at the Kolumbia Haus; it was
there that one SS NCO told the doomed stormtroop leader he roused
from his cell after midnight, 'Put your head under the tap so you look
fresh and make a good impression in death!'
From Munich and Berlin the blood-letting spread to the provinces;
in Silesia and the Grenzmark region manhunts of SA fugitives hiding
in the forests went on for days.
In Nazi parlance (as well as, oddly enough, in that of later German
historians) 30 June 1934 became known as the 'Röhm Putsch' – a
misnomer echoing Hitler's lie that 'a clique of perverts around
Röhm' had planned a coup in collusion with foreign powers. The
man in the street, on the other hand, called it the 'Night of the Long
Knives' and thereby hit on a phrase at once more accurate and more
graphic.
As the vapours cleared from the slaughterhouse scenes at Stadelheim
Prison and the Kolumbia Haus, it became apparent who had been the
wielders of the longest knives: the SS was raised – by an order of the
Führer dated 20 July 1934 – to the status of an autonomous organization within the Nazi Party and empowered to set up armoured units
of its own.
The latter reward posed an ominous paradox for the Reichswehr,
since it meant that no sooner had the challengers to its military monopoly been liquidated than the liquidators themselves presented the very
same challenge.
As for the SS, the Night of the Long Knives can be said to have
completed the chrysalis stage of its development. Hereafter the corporate personality of the Black Order remained fixed – despite the
evolution of its sub-groups into intelligence service, political police,
human bloodstock society, slave labour agency and Corps of Janissaries.
This protean role involved occasional mishaps – as when the murder
of Chancellor Dollfuss in July 1934 failed to precipitate a Nazi takeover

of Austria – but generally the progress of the SS was smooth and its scope limited only by Hitler's veto.

The first division of what ultimately became the wartime Waffen SS was raised – and accepted by a reluctant Reichswehr (now renamed Wehrmacht) – as part of conscription, which came into force in March 1935. This nucleus of the future SS army was given its own Sandhursts in the shape of the officer cadet schools at Bad Tölz and Brunswick, which were created by Paul Hausser, a retired Reichswehr Lieutenant-General and therefore the highest-ranking former regular officer ever to don the black uniform.

In April 1935 Himmler and Heydrich followed up their acquisition of an army with that of a newspaper, the *Schwarze Korps* (Black Guard) whose style – part-incantatory, part-prurient – soon attracted a mass readership. Besides adulation of Hitler and crudest Jew-baiting – the staples of Nazi journalism – the SS paper featured population-booster campaigns, attacks on wealth or privilege and directives for 'spontaneous' violence.

To boost the birth-rate it extolled motherhood irrespective of wed-lock, campaigned for diaper services and served up visual aphrodisiacs in the form of photographs of sunkissed bodies among waving ears of corn.

These inducements to procreation dovetailed with attacks on 'life-denying' morality and religion: throughout the Nazi campaign against Political Catholicism the *Schwarze Korps* produced riveting exposures of sexual and financial malpractices in monastic institutions.

From thus shocking the bourgeoisie it was but a short step to scourging them; each week the paper held up some factory boss for providing inadequate toilet facilities, or a farmer whose tied cottages had leaking roofs, to public obloquy. (This was a profitable crusade from which the *Schwarze Korps* earned political dividends and its editors financial ones – in the shape of conscience money from employers who preferred blackmail to scandal.)

Most importantly the paper provided a free information service for amateur lynch mobs. It did this by publishing names, addresses and (occasionally) photographs of individuals up and down the country guilty of non-contribution to the Winter Help charity, breaching the boycott of Jewish shops or refusing to tender the Hitler salute.

A noteworthy feature of the *Schwarze Korps* was its total lack of self-consciousness: marriage and birth announcements on the inside pages carried the by-line Dachau as if it were the most natural thing in the world for a maternity home to be next to a torture chamber. (Dachau concentration camp, aptly illustrating the Nazi ethos, contained SS married quarters.)

Although few SS men were even of early middle age, the paper's personal columns also regularly carried black-edged death notices. Fatal training mishaps, riding accidents, motor-cycle crashes – all reflected that other aspect of the SS ethos whereby the general effusion of blood was the only circumstance distinguishing a field of battle from a field of exercise.

If the SS upper age-limit was early middle age, the lower one came close to adolescence: *Schwarze Korps* editor, Günther d'Alquen, was all of twenty-three years of age at the time of his appointment to this key post. But as well as enjoying unprecedented scope for advancement, young SS men were subject to minute surveillance: d'Alquen, for instance, was ordered to break off an affair with a brown-eyed young lady and given three months in which to affiance himself to a possessor of blue irises, thus guaranteeing the eventual procreation of 100 per cent Nordic stock.

Painstaking checks of this type on the eugenic dossiers of intending SS brides were a chore Himmler still liked to undertake in person, even though within two years of the seizure of power SS membership had shot up from 52,000 to 165,000. The Reichsführer's prodigious pre-occupation with the Aryan myth made him lavish no less care on the past: he set up an *Ahnenerbe* ('Ancestral Heritage') institution to investigate Germanic prehistoric remains so as to establish the modern Germans' racial continuity with their forefathers. This institution, which operated under the aegis of a genuine professor of archaeology bearing the honorary rank of SS captain, with money donated by the big business 'Friendship Circle of the Reichsführer SS', sponsored large-scale excavations on sites in Germany, not to mention such bizarre adventures as an expedition to Tibet.

History – or to be more precise his own highly idiosyncratic version of it – gripped Himmler's imagination in an oddly personalized form. He was quite obsessed with the figure of Henry the Fowler, a tenth-century German king, on the anniversary of whose death he kept a yearly midnight tryst in the crypt of Quedlinburg Cathedral (the alleged site of the royal remains). At the millennium of Henry's death, 2 July 1936, Himmler vowed – before a band of Wehrmacht, Party and SS dignitaries bedecked with braid and medals – to continue and complete the anti-Slav crusade of the medieval monarch.

Mast-head of *Das Schwarze Korps* (The Black Guard), the official SS newspaper.

In private he carried the identification with his royal namesake (Henry = Heinrich) to even greater lengths; he claimed to commune with the dead king in his sleep and eventually looked upon himself as his reincarnation.

As if this was not enough, Himmler also viewed his own personality as big enough to accommodate the shade of King Arthur of Round Table fame: he had the derelict Wewelsburg Castle in Westphalia refurbished at considerable cost, and periodically assembled the twelve highest-ranking Obergruppenführer of the SS round the oaken table of its lofty dining-room. (On Himmler's orders each of the twelve wore a coat-of-arms of his own, and during his stay at the castle occupied a period-furnished chamber dedicated to a specific hero from German history.) The Wewelsburg's holy of holies was a subterranean shrine: plinths for the Obergruppenführers' cremation urns encircled a sunken well; on the death of each Knight of the Round Table his escutcheon was burnt on top of a hollowed-out stone pillar, with the smoke – by means of a cunningly arranged ventilation system – forming a vertical column above the well.

Similar rituals, though naturally less expensive and involved, formed the basis of the religion all SS men were expected to practise. 'Religion' is actually a misnomer, however, since it implies something of an altogether higher order than the hotchpotch of Teutonic ancestor worship and nature-cult that catered for the spiritual needs of the Nazi élite. The most pronounced characteristic of this New Heathenism was a rejection of almost every aspect of Christianity, ranging from the virtues of humility and charity to the symbolism of the cross.

The mystery of the Resurrection yielded to the eternal renewal of the race, otherworldliness to hero myths, and Christmas (with its date brought forward to the winter solstice) to Yule-tide.

'On the day of the winter solstice,' according to an SS manual, 'the
sun rises again from its wintry grave. This annual event was cele-
brated as the greatest festival of our forbears. They advanced towards
the Yule-night with firebrands to liberate the sun from the bondage
of wintry death, and thought of it as a young hero come to rouse and
free them from their death-like sleep. . . . On Christmas Eve the main
ingredients of the festive fare must be carp, roast goose and wild
boar – drawn respectively from the sphere of water, air and earth. At
the conclusion of the meal the father uses the Yule candleholder to
kindle the lights on the Yule-tree, leaving three candles unlit. The
other members of family and clan are summoned and the father
kindles the remaining three candles, saying: "This light shall burn
in memory of our ancestors who are with us today. This light shall
burn for my dead comrades from the war and the time of struggle,
and this light shall burn to remind us of all our German brethren
across the globe celebrating Christmas with us today!" '

Yule-tide involved the use of such ritual objects as Yule-plates,
wreaths and wheels. The plates, made of zinc, wood or earthenware
and sometimes engraved with the tree-shaped life-rune, were actually
all-purpose bowls, and as such could be filled with presents at
Christmas, coloured eggs at Easter, apples at harvest thanksgiving, and
bread and salt at weddings. Yule wreaths of riband-garlanded fir-twigs
were either hung vertically as Advent wreaths or suspended horizontally
from an upright wooden pole wedged into the hub of a Yule wheel (its
six symmetrical spokes symbolized the intersection of the horizon with
the diagonals formed by the terminal points of the sun's orbit at the
winter and summer solstice in German latitudes).

The manual went on: 'After the exchange of the presents the family
listens to the Christmas broadcast of the Deputy of the Führer.
Thereafter – in view of the fact that Yule-tide is the greatest clan
festival – it is becoming customary to look at old family photographs,
recount old family stories and to exchange ideas about the success of
the steadily deepening research into family genealogies.'

In its treatment of death the SS 'catechism' alternated mock-
profundities with minute *pompes funèbres* regulations:

'Just as vernal resurrection belongs to life so does autumnal decease.
Being born and dying are part of life. Because all life is sacred to us,
birth and death too are indefeasible – hence funeral rites belong to
the annual cycle of our festivals. . . . Conveyance to the cemetery

requires a horsedrawn flat carriage affording maximum view of the SS flag-draped coffin topped by the dagger and peaked cap of the deceased. (The carriage is to be adorned with fir-twigs and the horses are on no account to be caparisoned in black.) After speeches at the graveside the dead SS man's unit-commander exchanges the dagger on top of the coffin for that of one of the next-of-kin – symbol of the latter's assumption of his dead comrade's obligation to strive and struggle. When the coffin is lowered the SS men present form a circle round the grave and – in military posture – intone the SS *Treuelied* [hymn of loyalty].'

Himmler may have imagined himself to be King Arthur and Henry the Fowler incarnate; in reality he was Nazism's Duke of Alba crossed with Ignatius Loyola, and his SS doubled as a Council of Blood and as a monastic order defending the true faith. The analogy with the Jesuits even holds good in education – though with the difference that whereas Loyola had wanted to concentrate on a child's first seven years, the SS were directly involved in educating the ten-plus age group.

Since the German school system had shown strong traces of authoritarianism even under the Weimar Republic, the Nazis felt little need for drastic reform. Their main innovation consisted of the setting-up of two public (i.e. boarding) school networks: the 'Napolas' (*National Politische Erziehungsanstalten* or National Political Educational Institutions) for the training of officers and government functionaries, and the *Adolf Hitler Schulen* in which the next generation of Party and SS leaders was to be reared. (The *Hitler Schulen* were wholly, and the Napolas partly, controlled by the SS.)

The selection of pupils took place at ten, according to partly medical and partly aesthetic criteria: anyone below A1 fitness (such as spectacle wearers) or of insufficiently Nordic appearance was excluded. Applications for admission originated – independently of parents' wishes – from the Hitler Youth, which also tested candidates' 'leadership potential' at special selection-camps which they had to attend for a fortnight.

At the *Adolf Hitler Schulen* sport enjoyed virtual parity with academic subjects and occupied two-fifths of the timetable. Religious Instruction – still in the curriculum at ordinary schools – was replaced by 'Political Studies', i.e. the regurgitation of *Völkische Beobachter* editorials and news reports. The great watchword was 'Kameradschaft': pupils used the informal 'Du' when addressing teachers, whose desks stood at floor level instead of on the raised platform customary in German classrooms. Even more novel was the absence of such standard means of evaluating pupils as tests and exams. In consequence no subject grades appeared on end-of-year reports; the only information conveyed related to the pupil's degree of leadership potential. Classes were called 'platoons', and outside the classroom the running of the schools largely devolved on Hitler Youth NCOs.

Each year a fixed quota of *Adolf Hitler Schulen* alumni graduated to the Party's 'finishing schools' or *Ordensburgen*, at which sport and military training of Spartan severity predominated (and produced a commensurate casualty rate). However, the *Ordensburgen* – not to be confused with the officer-training schools of the military SS – came under the control of the Party's Political Organization, which meant that the (non-military) future SS leadership would in fact have had a less than 100 per cent SS education.

This confusing overlap of Party and SS educational fiefs was paralleled in membership. To back his claim that the SS was synonymous with Nazi Germany's élite, Himmler awarded honorary *Ehrenführer* titles to highly-placed Party and government officials. These titles meant little but they did produce the bizarre situation whereby implacable personal enemies of Himmler like Martin Bormann and Foreign Minister Ribbentrop held nominal commissions in the SS.

Top-ranking scientists and academics were similarly honoured, though the *Bildungsbürgertum* (educated bourgeoisie) as such hardly required this sort of bait: no fewer than 12,000 representatives of the 'liberal professions' (half of them lawyers and doctors) enrolled voluntarily in the Black Order. In addition so many scions of the nobility donned the Death's Head uniform – modelled, incidentally, on the pages' livery at the Bavarian court – that in places the list of the SS officer establishment read like the German counterpart of *Burke's Peerage*.

Though only one German in 134 bore the aristocratic prefix *von*, the blue-blooded proportion among the SS Obergruppenführer (full generals) was one in five, among the SS Gruppenführer (lieutenant-generals) one in ten and among the SS Brigadeführer (major-generals) one in seven.

Some of these titled recruits conferred more than mere aristocratic glamour on their new knightly order – the 'SA hunters' von dem

Exemplary Nazi paterfamilias: Himmler with his daughter Gudrun at an indoor sports meeting in Berlin (1938)

SS top brass in full ceremonial panoply. Himmler (left), Heydrich (middle), Karl Wolff (front right)

A study in contrasts:
Himmler, the would-be sportsman

Heydrich, the champion fencer

The rivals: SA chief of staff Roehm and SS boss Himmler, four months before their lethal clash in 1934

The Burning of the Books in 1933. SA and SS men preparing for the auto-da-fe

Bach-Zelewski and von Woyrsch had both held army commissions and seen service in the Freikorps.

A key section of the SS leadership consisted of well-born desperadoes whom a combination of post-war circumstances and personal inadequacy had kept from their appointed station in life. The wartime Higher SS and Police leader in Poland, Friedrich Wilhelm Krüger, a colonel's son, was a failed businessman; Himmler's liaison officer with Hitler, Karl Wolff, a judge's son, had run an unsuccessful advertising agency; and the subsequent Higher SS and Police leader in Occupied France, Carl Albrecht Oberg, was a doctor's son whose banana import business had gone bankrupt.

Alongside *déclassé* aristocrats and bourgeois who had gone off the rails, the SS command accommodated selected well-publicized individuals risen from the lower depths of society. One such was the *Leibstandarte* commandant and subsequent Waffen SS general, Sepp Dietrich, a coarse-featured, squat man exuding peasant brutality. The illegitimate son of a Bavarian farmhand, Dietrich had been intended for the butcher's trade – a choice of career to which this Great War sergeant-major was to remain true for the rest of his life.

The social group most attuned to the spirit of the age were the unsentimental SD intellectuals enjoying unprecedented career opportunities as Himmler's social engineers and programmers of genocide.

Of these Otto Ohlendorf could well be described as first among equals. The career of this bright young economist with an – unfulfilled – postgraduate ambition to found an institute for the study of Nazism spanned the creation of SD Internal Intelligence, command of an *Einsatzgruppe* (killer commando unit) in Southern Russia and control of a department at the Foreign Trade Ministry.

Ohlendorf's colleague Dr Franz Six rose from being in charge of SD *Kultur* activities (at the age of twenty-seven) to the professorship of Politics at Berlin University and a top desk at the Foreign Ministry. *En route* Six held two 'shadow' appointments: SD chief designate for Occupied Britain and head of the SD task force detailed to secure occupied Moscow. (The main guidelines for his British posting were contained in a death list of two thousand names, headed by CHURCHILL, Winston Spencer.)

Then there was Walter Schellenberg, student of both law and medicine at Bonn University, who rose within seven years from apprentice spy to major-general and had by the age of thirty-two become head of SD Foreign Intelligence.

The SD – originally the Party's internal police and intelligence service – had by 1936 so enlarged its area of competence that the Wehrmacht was forced to negotiate a 'treaty' with it to demarcate their respective spheres of foreign espionage. This treaty (known as the 'Ten Commandments') allocated political intelligence work to the SD and its military counterpart to the Army's *Abwehr* under Admiral Canaris.

One of the SD's sensational though fortuitous espionage successes of this period related to the downfall of Marshal Tuchatschewsky, the Russian deputy Defence Commissar. Towards the end of 1936 Heydrich had heard – via foreign SD sources – of Red Army schemes for a *coup d'état* involving Marshal Tuchatschewsky, and he decided to forward forged documents to Stalin implicating the Marshal in treasonable contacts with Germany. Heydrich's design to precipitate a clash between Stalin and the Russian military leaders was facilitated by Tuchatschewsky's previous collaboration – under the terms of Russo-German agreements of the 1920s – with high-ranking Reichswehr officers.

When in June 1937 *Tass* reported the execution of Tuchatschewsky and seven Russian generals – prelude to a purge involving half the Red Army's officer corps – Heydrich claimed the credit for this auspicious *dénouement*. Though the claim was widely accepted among those privy to the affair, *Abwehr* chief Canaris dissented; a thorough analysis of the time-factors involved convinced him that the liquidation of Tuchatschewsky had been a long premeditated action on Stalin's part in which Heydrich's planted evidence was of no more than marginal importance.

This realization eventually led Canaris to the conclusion that the mendacity and amateurism of the expanding SD *Apparat* was endangering Germany's military security – a conclusion that brought in its train endemic friction between Wehrmacht and SS. But before the SD became involved in a straightforward contretemps with the military, there occurred a bizarre episode which illuminated the SS relationship with a much more powerful institution than the Army – namely the Party.

The economics expert Ohlendorf had built up an SD commercial intelligence network feeding data on business and labour trends to the government departments concerned. After a while he had switched from economic to political fact-finding with a particular emphasis on the state of public opinion in the Reich. In this the SS idealist - and subsequent mass-murderer – Ohlendorf was motivated by the reformist notion that the spotlighting of abuses might produce an improvement.

Early in 1938 the SD inflicted two consecutive – and cumulative – blows on the Army. In this, however, they acted less as initiators of policy than as executors, since essentially they only 'produced' the evidence which Hitler required to topple War Minister Blomberg and Army commander-in-chief Fritsch.

These two had been among half a dozen key figures to whom Hitler had in November 1937 divulged his plans for the forcible incorporation of Austria and Czechoslovakia and a premeditated collision with the West. Blomberg's and Fritsch's unenthusiastic response to this plan caused Hitler to cast around for a pretext on which they could be dismissed without alienating the rest of the military caste.

Heydrich was able to oblige almost instantly, since his unmatched weapon in the bitter infighting that passed for normalcy at the top level of the Nazi society consisted of incriminating dossiers – compiled with the aid of thousands of agents – on every person of any consequence in the Reich.

Blomberg, a widower in his sixties, had married a typist half his age. Within weeks of this *mésalliance* the SD produced documents implicating the second Frau Blomberg in modelling for blue photographs and her mother in running a call-girl service. The SD revelations caused the Field Marshal to lose caste among the military high-ups to whom they had been communicated and forced him into an early retirement.

The Fritsch affair was both more complex and more protracted. It hinged on an arrested blackmailer who claimed to have extorted money from the general by threatening to divulge his homosexuality. Fritsch denied the allegations on oath and was given indefinite leave while a military court of honour investigated them.

The deliberations of the court were interrupted by the invasion of Austria – which had been one of the main points at issue between Hitler and Blomberg and Fritsch. After the *Anschluss* (when it no longer mattered) the court established that the blackmailer had confused the general with a homosexual cavalry captain called von Frisch and had been forced to persist in his charge under threat of Gestapo torture. Though exonerated Fritsch was not reappointed – a slight he eventually expiated by his death in the Polish campaign of September 1939.

The purge of the army leadership in February 1938 had marked the beginning of the openly belligerent phase of Nazi policy. The subsequent twelve months saw – in breathtaking succession – the Austrian

Anschluss (March 1938), the incorporation of the Sudetenland (October 1938), the horrendous *Kristallnacht* pogrom (November 1938), and the annexation of rump-Czechoslovakia (March 1939); events which, besides giving the SS a greater share in foreign policy, drastically changed the scale and nature of the concentration camp system.

One of Himmler's pre-eminent concerns (as 'Commissioner for the Consolidation of German Folkdom') was safeguarding the *Deutschtum* of Germans outside the Reich, and the SS had had a stake in Austria since their abortive July 1934 putsch in which Chancellor Dollfuss had been killed. When Dollfuss' successor Dr Schuschnigg yielded to Hitler's ultimatum on 11 March 1938 and let the Wehrmacht march in, the German and Austrian SS dovetailed their activities with terrifying effectiveness.

Foolproof security arrangements operated during Hitler's triumphal 'homecoming'; within weeks 79,000 arrests took place in Vienna, whence freight trains crowded with human cargo departed regularly for Dachau and other concentration camps. A savage persecution of the Jews drove more than half of the two-hundred-thousand-strong community out of the country before the outbreak of war; in fact it is hardly an exaggeration to state that the Nazification of Austria – eagerly abetted by the local population – took the same number of months as that of Germany had taken years.

The chief local executors of SS policy were Ernst Kaltenbrunner, Odilo Globocnik and Adolf Eichmann – three men whose peers would be hard to find in the annals of inhumanity.

Kaltenbrunner, a hulking scar-faced lawyer with hands which reminded Schellenberg of a gorilla's, eventually succeeded Heydrich and became one of the chief accused at Nuremberg; the ex-convict Globocnik, notorious for dynamiting a Jewish jeweller's, lived in blood and corruption as his natural habitat; the Dachau trainee Eichmann was to reduce mankind by several million during the war – in the interim he terrorized Viennese and (after March 1939) Czech Jews into saving themselves by flight as best they could.

The material and labour resources thus appropriated during 1938-9 prompted a change in the scale as well as the nature of the concentration camps. With an influx of Austrians, Jews and Czechs swelling the camp population, the KZ network had proliferated into close on a hundred centres of varying size by mid-1939. Besides the prototype camp at Dachau – which with its ancillaries eventually accommodated a wartime maximum of anything between 25,000 and 60,000 inmates – there was

Sachsenhausen-Oranienburg with fifteen ancillary work-camps (20–35,000 inmates), Buchenwald with eighty (20–50,000), Flossenburg with fifteen (30–40,000), the *Frauenlager* ('women's camp'), at Ravensbruck, with twenty (15–30,000), and Mauthausen with fifteen (40–70,000).

Before the annexation of Austria, concentration-camp labour had been largely employed in the construction and enlargement of the camps themselves and of the adjacent SS buildings. After the *Anschluss* Himmler decided to use his unprecedented labour resources as a new source of enrichment and economic power. To the expropriation of the wealth of Jewish inmates (which the SS either confiscated outright or acquired through blackmail and the solicitation of bribes) he added a higher dimension of profitability by the impressment of prison labour in quarrying, road-building and other construction work, market gardening, handicrafts, and (later on) the manufacture of armaments.

Even though the guards would contrive to make the apparently most innocuous assignments lethal – emaciated 'market gardeners' man-handling heavy wheelbarrows would be beaten when they stumbled, and sometimes drowned in pits of liquid manure – a prisoner's chances of survival naturally varied according to the nature of his work. Assignment to quarrying and construction work was tantamount to a briefly suspended death sentence, whilst handicraft jobs – particularly those catering to the needs of SS camp personnel – might even procure privileges for individual prisoner craftsmen.

This informal grading of labour tasks according to the mortal hazards involved had its official counterpart on a different plane. Eicke's KZ administration classified all *Lager* under its control on a threefold scale of ascending severity – with I denoting 'soft', II 'medium' and III 'tough' camps. On Eicke's scale Dachau represented the soft end of the spectrum(!) while category III was exemplified by Mauthausen, the death camp in Upper Austria built after the *Anschluss* to accommodate Viennese Jews. (Despite this designation, Mauthausen differed from the rationalized death camps set up subsequently in occupied Poland because in it the infliction of death had not yet reached the level of industrial processing.)

Mauthausen had been a stone quarry on the edge of the picturesque Salzkammergut lake region near Salzburg; conversion into a KZ meant levelling a wooded hillside and building huge granite walls. Within the circle of megaliths, death was applied by pre-industrial means: SS guards would push human chains of prisoners over the precipitous edges of the quarry – a practice which so disconcerted the civilian quarry workers who had been kept on that they complained to the camp administration about the unsightliness of the human remains bespattering the rock face.

Having gained a virtual stranglehold on Czechoslovakia through the *Anschluss*, Hitler spent the spring and summer of 1938 exacerbating the conflict between the Czechs and their (largely Nazified) Sudeten-German minority. In these manœuvres the SS played a considerable part: the strings jerking the puppet-like Sudeten Gauleiter Henlein were pulled by the *Volksdeutsche Mittelstelle* (Volksdeutsche Liaison Office, VOMI for short), the SS special agency for Germans living outside the Reich.

Flashpoint had nearly been reached in September 1938, when the West appeased Hitler at Munich by agreeing to the partial dismember-ment of Czechoslovakia. Under the Munich treaty the torso of the Czech state was further weakened by the granting of autonomy to a Slovak provincial government at Bratislava.

In early March 1939 the SD resumed its foreign policy initiative: a 'trouble-shooter' unit under Alfred Naujocks arranged a series of bomb explosions in the Slovak capital which provoked a rift between Prague and Bratislava and thus provided Hitler with a pretext for invading and obliterating the rest of Czechoslovakia.

Five months later an appreciative Führer cast his SD trouble-shooters in a leading role: the flames they kindled were to provide a farcical overture to world conflagration. On 31 August 1939 Naujocks's men, wearing Polish army uniforms, raided the German radio trans-mitter at Gleiwitz (Silesia), fired a few shots in the air, broadcast a Polish proclamation and departed – leaving behind a dead 'Pole' (actually the corpse of a German concentration-camp inmate in Polish battledress) to lend a touch of verisimilitude to the proceedings. Next morning Hitler, in a Reichstag speech, announced the invasion of Poland as a retaliatory move 'provoked' by the Gleiwitz raid and a host of similar fake attacks carried out by the SD.

The Naujocks type of operation had by then become standard SD practice, it would barely deserve mention but for Hitler's attempt to inflate it into the Sarajevo of the Second World War.

Rather less routine was the Venlo incident in neutral Holland which occurred some weeks after the end of the Polish campaign. An osten-sibly anti-Nazi German émigré – who in fact worked for the SD – had inveigled Captain Payne-Best and Major Stevens of British Military Intelligence into a rendezvous with Schellenberg at the Dutch-German

border town of Venlo, whence Schellenberg (with covering fire from
Naujocks's unit) audaciously abducted them in broad daylight. This
coup brought rewards for all concerned: Schellenberg was promoted to
SS Major-General (and head of SD External Intelligence eighteen
months later) and the SD acquired greater leverage in foreign policy
through the elevation of the heads of its various foreign networks into –
diplomatically immune – Police Attachés at German embassies.

Even so Himmler had good reason for viewing the Venlo incident
with mixed feelings. Hitler, who later – in Spring 1940 – adduced
Stevens's and Payne-Best's presence in Holland as proof of Dutch-
Allied collusion justifying his invasion of the neutral Netherlands, had
placed a different construction on it at the time of the actual kidnapping.
The 'incident' happened to occur on the same day – 8 November 1939 –
as an unsuccessful bomb attempt on his life (at the Munich beer cellar
where the Party old guard assembled annually in commemoration of the
1923 Putsch) and this coincidence convinced Hitler of a connection
between the British and the bomb.

The man solely responsible for the Munich explosion – as the police
soon established – had in fact been a lone wolf German anti-Nazi by the
name of Elser, who was caught trying to cross illegally into Switzerland
a few hours later. Hitler, however, was so convinced that his would-be
assassin was merely the man-of-straw of a widely ramified conspiracy
involving Britain, the Jews, the Freemasons and the German Resistance,
that he ordered the Gestapo to extract the truth from Elser (and also
from Stevens and Payne-Best) by all the considerable means at its
disposal.

After the veteran investigator, Kripa Chief Nebe, had failed to dis-
lodge Elser from his claim to sole authorship of the bomb plot, it fell
to the furiously embarrassed Himmler to extract the confession
demanded by Hitler. Screaming abuse he hurled himself upon the
trussed-up prisoner to kick him repeatedly in the chest, stomach and
groin, and had him beaten into unconsciousness several times and
thereafter brought round with jets of cold water – but to equally little
avail.

The fruitlessness of this investigation markedly, if temporarily,
lowered Himmler's standing in the eyes of Hitler – a fact that was not
lost on Ribbentrop and sundry high-ranking enemies of the Reichsführer
– but also paradoxically saved Elser's life since Himmler did not want
to sever his only link with the supposed instigators of the conspiracy.
Elser was accordingly transferred to Dachau, where he was given an

assignment that saved him from exposure to the maltreatment and overwork general throughout the camp.

Even so, Elser may not have noticed that at Dachau nesting-birds were objects of the SS guards' special solicitude; just as it is doubtful whether any inmate concerned knew that the SS had made Goethe's favourite oak tree in the vicinity of Weimar their central point in the planning of Buchenwald concentration camp. One of Mauthausen's distinctive features were the curling roofs of the guardhouses on top of its granite walls – a deliberate pastiche of the guardhouses along the Great Wall of China.

These bizarre touches reflected the sentimental aestheticism which occasionally rose to the surface of the Nazi mind; among its best-known manifestations were the compulsory singing of (often specially commissioned) KZ songs by inmates and the creation of a camp orchestra whose music, broadcast over loudspeakers, provided a monstrous counterpoint to the camps' everyday sounds of toil, violence and pain.

Hitler bathed his emotions in the surging cadences of Wagner, Heydrich shone at private chamber music recitals, and Governor Hans Frank of Poland would make the Baroque spaces of Cracow's Wawel Palace echo with nocturnal piano–playing. But Himmler was a creature utterly devoid of artistic accomplishment. His aesthetic tastes were amply catered for by the commandant's house at Stutthof concentration camp (near the prewar Polish border) where he occasionally stayed after hunting trips on East Prussian estates. It was a sandstone house – white, clean and rectangular with wrought-iron grilles. At night, whilst the lethal current crackled in the barbed wire encircling the camp, the somnolent Reichsführer's ear would catch the rustling of the nearby pine forests and the distant murmur of the sea.

3

Schoolmasters
and Spies

A PHOTOGRAPH OF HIMMLER'S CLASS AT LANDSHUT GYMNASIUM
shows a group of senior boys in multi-coloured caps and sashes who can
be seen gripping the crooks of their walking-sticks like sabre hilts. The
aura which these self-consciously haughty eighteen-year-olds exude
compounds menace with *Romantik* – exalted romanticism being then
very much in vogue among the educated young.

Himmler's lifelong penchant for *Romantik* – during the trial of
General Fritsch before a military honour court he assembled twelve
SS dignitaries in an adjacent room and bade them concentrate their
minds to influence the general into telling the truth – accounted for the
Schutzstaffeln exhibiting even wilder contradictions than other Party
formations.

Thus the Black Order which ran a slave labour empire producing
colossal profits forbade its members to acquire goods on hire purchase,
which Himmler believed was a capitalistic vice. The barracks of the
militarized SS were furnished with wardrobes and cupboards which
could not be locked – to instil comradeship into recruits who were at
the same time adjured to report each other's political (or sexual) devia-
tions. Concentration camp guards were warned against wasteful use of
firearms on the grounds that each bullet cost the Reich three pfennigs –
the inference being that prisoners' lives were worth even less – yet they
had to sign statements every three months to the effect that they knew
they must not maltreat prisoners.

If during basic training SS recruits dropped the cartridges they were
loading into chargers, they had to pick them off the ground with their
teeth; for the most trifling slip they had to do fifty knee-bends with
rifles held out at arm's length – yet, having been reduced to bundles of
jerking limbs without a will of their own, they were subsequently raised
to lords over death and creation.

And just like Olympian deities SS men exuded physical prowess and
youth. Heydrich represented the Reich at international fencing contests

and SS riders swept the board at German equestrian events. D'Alquen, the editor of the *Schwarze Korps* had not yet reached thirty when the circulation of his weekly (initial printing: seventy thousand) reached a peak of three-quarters of a million copies.

It took Heinz Reinefarth four years to rise to general of police; Kurt Meyer, nicknamed 'Panzer-Meyer' became – at the age of thirty-three – the youngest divisional commander in German military history. Himmler himself was only thirty-four when he took command of the combined German police forces and the Gestapo.

With his peering eyes, weak chin and sloping shoulders Himmler projected a rather unprepossessing image, but Heydrich – athlete, fencer, pilot, leader of military SS route marches – undeniably made up for the deficiencies of his superior. Nothing illustrated the two men's complementary qualities more clearly than the contribution each made to the sphere of Nazi fencing: while Heydrich garnered trophies, Himmler devised the SS duelling *reglement* which laid down, among other things, under what special circumstances the preliminaries to an *affaire d'honneur* could be conducted by registered post.

This not untypical attention to detail had a positive influence on the standing of the SS among a nation inclined to invest meticulousness with moral significance. While some Germans viewed Himmler's *Apparat* with unconcealed horror, others saw it as a repository of order and a deterrent against corruption. When during the war, in which corruption mushroomed, Himmler amassed ever more power, many Germans rationalized their apprehension at this development by interpreting it as a portent of the cleansing postwar purge to come.

The Black Order was well aware of the ambivalent feelings it aroused. As early as 1934 Himmler had stated with unusual candour: 'We know that some Germans feel ill at the sight of the black uniform and we don't expect to be loved.' The SS certainly never did anything to solicit love – but while disdaining to court popularity, they frequently earned the public's shuddering respect.

Thus during the *Kristallnacht* (the nation-wide orgy of anti-Jewish arson and vandalism in November 1938) the half-horrified, half-fascinated watching crowds could not but marvel at the efficiency with which the stage-managers of the SS pogrom prevented the destruction of Jewish property from affecting adjacent German property.

(Not only Germans came to marvel at the foresight of the SS. In April 1943 all Poles living within a mile radius of the Warsaw Ghetto

The wire-puller. Typical Nazi election poster depicting Jewish manipulation of the economy and public life.

were instructed to keep their windows open to prevent the panes shattering while Brigadeführer's Stroop's men dynamited the last crumbling Jewish dwellings.)

Beside meticulousness and foresight the Black Order placed considerable emphasis on smartness – both in the martial and the sartorial sense of the term. No state occasion in the Third Reich was complete without a steel-helmeted SS guard of honour with gleaming black jackboots and black dress uniforms with white insignia and piping. White-gloved and peak-capped SS subalterns also formed part of the décor at all Nazi social occasions, great or small. They would be found escorting screen starlets at Berlin's glittering annual *Filmball* (which Hitler took delight in honouring with his presence) or pouring the coffee and passing the pastries when the proletarian Frau Gauleiter Koch entertained the ladies of East Prussia's landed aristocracy.

True to its deep-seated ambivalence, the same Black Order that lent a touch of urbanity to Nazi social life also aimed to settle its members as farmers-in-arms (*Wehrbauern*) in Eastern Europe and promoted a cult of peasant simplicity in house and furniture design completely at variance with the décor of the *Filmball*.

The fittings and furnishings of the ideal SS house comprised heavy roof beams with metal mountings, unstained rustic furniture, hand-woven Frisian wool hangings, wrought-iron candelabra, earthenware jugs, pewter table utensils and, the centre of attraction, a rough-hewn wooden cradle – preferably hand-carved by the paterfamilias in person.

Equally rough-hewn was the Nazi approach to population growth – officially termed *Geburtenschlacht* (battle of births). As chief strategist of the battle of births Himmler deplored the low fertility of many German marriages and the widespread taboo, both social and religious, on illegitimate motherhood. The war eventually enabled him to by-pass these obstacles by the *Eindeutschung* or Germanization of Nordic-looking Slavs, i.e. by biological kidnapping; but even earlier his own SS had provided volunteer 'procreation assistants' for single women eager for motherhood.

All the pieces in Himmler's eugenic jigsaw – infertile couples, Germanized Slavs, 'procreation assistants', unmarried mothers – were moved into place by 'Lebensborn' (Fountain of Life), an SS foundling hospital-cum-adoption society established in 1936. According to the Lebensborn report for 1938, '832 valuable German women decided despite their single state and the sacrifice entailed, to eschew abortion and present the nation with a child'. Assessing each German's life contribution to the economy at one hundred thousand Reichsmark, Lebensborn claimed to have enriched the country by eighty-three million Reichsmark.

Eventually thousands of Lebensborn wards were placed with childless Nazi couples; more importantly, in wartime the original objective – delivering and fostering illegitimate German children – was superseded by the genetic spoliation of Eastern Europe.

During his first inspection tour of occupied Poland Himmler had been deeply stirred by the Nordic appearance of many Slav children and this may have started a train of thought culminating in his war aim 'to enlarge Germany's existing blood basis of 90 million to 120 million'. Kidnapped children – snatched from orphanages or alleged resistance families – were taken to Lebensborn homes dotted across occupied Europe; after a processing period during which the bewildered children were drilled in rudimentary German and denied any contact with their compatriots, they went off to the Reich already bearing the names of their designated foster parents.

Germanization was by no means confined to children nor were all Germanized Slavs necessarily outright victims of force. In Poland, where Poles and Germans had long intermarried, Polish nationals of part-German ancestry could apply for Reich citizenship which – given the situation of Poles under Nazi occupation – many were quite eager to do.

But volunteers could never meet Himmler's need for genetic reinforcements, and two special SS agencies – the Volkdeutsche Liaison Office and the Race and Settlement Office – scoured Europe to select human specimens considered suitable for Germanization. Besides abduction, the tasks of RUSHA, the Race and Settlement Office, ranged from conscription of slave labour, the infliction of (frequently capital) punishment on East Europeans guilty of intimacy with German women, to the clearance of Slavs from regions earmarked for German settlement.

One such region was the Warthegau in Western Poland. The Warthegau 'plantation' involved clearing one and a half million Poles and Jews out of a large area to make room for half a million *Volksdeutsche* from Eastern Poland, Rumania and the Baltic States. Himmler, newly styled 'Reich Commissioner for the consolidation of German folkdom', ordered the clearance during the Arctic winter of 1939–40, and thus caused a heavier death toll than resulted from Hitler's concurrent directive to decapitate the Polish nation by liquidating its intellectuals and priests.

These SS population transfers resembled nothing so much as the fourth-century Migration of the Peoples. Like their precursors in the Dark Ages, they were characterized in equal parts by barbarity and chaos: in 1942 Germans from Yugoslavia arrived in the East Polish areas whence *Volksdeutsche* had migrated to the Warthegau two years earlier.

The migrants, apart from having to give up ancient homesteads, frequently in exchange for makeshift accommodation in transit camps, were never asked whether or where they wanted to move; 'beneficiaries' and victims of the population transfers alike simply served the grand design of enlarging and consolidating the area of German settlement in Europe.

A related aim – that of purifying the gene pool of the German race – lay behind the Euthanasia Campaign of 1940-1. In September 1939 Hitler ordered the 'mercy-killing' of the feeble-minded and incurables throughout the Reich – on grounds both of eugenics and wartime economy in food, accommodation and medical personnel. The first liquidation centre became operational before the end of the year; another five, one of them situated at the well-known psychiatric clinic of Hadamar, came into operation early in 1940. The man placed in overall charge of the programme was Christian Wirth, the former superintendent of the Criminal Investigation Department in Stuttgart.

Wirth initially disposed of his victims by shooting them in the neck. After some time he switched over to gassing them in specially constructed chambers – and thus qualifies as co-originator of the mass-extermination methods subsequently used in the so-called 'Final Solution of the Jewish Question'.

In each euthanasia establishment a room camouflaged as a shower-room was hermetically sealed. This was connected by a system of pipes to cylinders of carbon monoxide. The patients, before being taken in groups of ten or fifteen into this gas chamber, were generally made drowsy with the aid of morphine (or scopolamine) injections or drugged with soporifics. Each centre housed a crematorium; families were informed of patients' deaths on pre-printed forms attributing death to heart failure or pneumonia.

The steep increase in fatalities, reported under conditions of ill-concealed secrecy – palls of smoke above the crematoria were visible for miles, and at Hadamar the village children would greet incoming hospital buses with cries of 'here come some more to be gassed' – prompted mounting disquiet in the country. Among many rumours in circulation

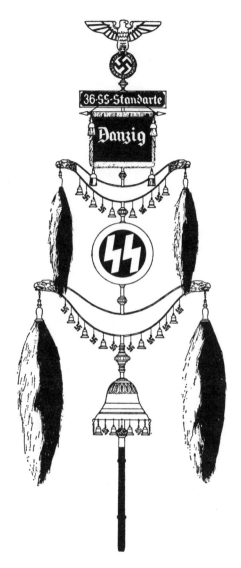

A Jingling Johnny used by SS military bands.

was one which alleged that even badly wounded soldiers were being 'mercy-killed' at military hospitals.

In August 1941 the Catholic Bishop Galen denounced the euthanasia killings in a sermon from the pulpit of his cathedral at Münster, Westphalia. This turned out to be the most successful single act of resistance ever undertaken in the Third Reich: the systematic killing of institution inmates (which had thus far cost approximately a hundred thousand lives) ceased almost immediately.

Nor was any retaliatory action taken against the bishop, although the Gestapo soon afterwards beheaded three parish priests who had distributed his sermon in leaflet form. Such glaring discrepancy of punishment was the fruit of Machiavellian calculation: while the death of anonymous parish priests would go unremarked in the surrounding welter of violence and confusion, persecution might have elevated the well-known prelate to the status of a national resistance figure.

SS caps (*top*, other ranks 1934; *centre*, officers' standard model; *bottom*, other ranks 1935), and field cap badges (*top*, 1934; *bottom*, 1935)

SS uniforms (left, SS man in service dress; centre, SS man in winter service dress; right, SS officer in walking-out dress)

Formal evening dress for SS officers, 1938.

SS standard bearer's gorget (1938)

SS officer's dagger (1936)

SS drill: 'dressing from the right'

Changing the guard outside the old Reich chancellery (1935)

A medical for recruits of the SS *Verfügungstruppe* (1938)

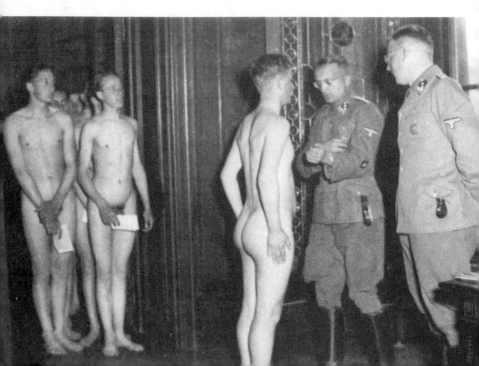

A meet in 1935. SS riders made a distinct contribution to 'high life' in the Third Reich

Hitler's 50th birthday

SS men partner Nazi maidens at a dancing display

Prescribed off-duty reading: *Das Schwarze Korps*

Nazi architecture
the refectory at
Ordensburg
Sonthofen, a
finishing school
for Nazi leaders

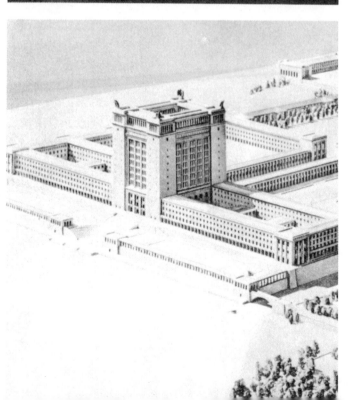

Nazi architecture:
design for a High
School

4

The SS at War

CONSIDERATIONS OF 'IMAGE' ALSO PLAYED A PART IN PROMPTING changes in the role of the SS. Since Himmler's 'admission' that many Germans felt ill at the sight of the black uniform, though not for that reason, black had ceased to be exclusively associated with the SS in the public mind. The *Verfügungstruppe* (military SS) under their *Inspekteur* Paul Hausser wore field-grey uniforms only distinguishable from Wehrmacht issue by SS insignia and badges of rank. (It was this uniform, incidentally, which Hitler wore – and swore not to take off till victory – when he announced the invasion of Poland to the Reichstag on 1 September 1939.)

Though the Polish campaign had already seen some military participation by the *Verfügungstruppe*, in the early part of the war, Hitler still essentially ascribed security functions to the SS. In August 1940 he stated that a centralized militarized police force with an efficient listening service could have prevented Germany's collapse in 1918. Six months later he opined: 'to keep the trust of a soldierly nation the SS need to shed their blood'; by the winter of 1941–2 – when Germany suffered its first reverses of the war on the Eastern front – it had become 'necessary to send the SS to the front to maintain their prestige'.

These dicta of the Führer's reflected various pressures set up by the changing fortunes of war. While on the one hand mounting casualty figures increased popular resentment of deskbound Nazi warriors – Party and SS officials 'on special duty', and thus exempt from front-line service – on the other hand the SS leadership saw the escalation of the War as an opportunity for levering the Wehrmacht out of its position of military monopoly.

Thus Hitler eventually sanctioned (in the historian Gerald Reitlinger's apt phrase) 'the messy infiltration of the SS into the army'. As an initial pointer towards the transformation of the *Verfügungstruppe* into a thorough-going SS army, the title 'Waffen SS' was introduced in January 1940. When later that year the SS *Verfügungstruppe* Inspectorate became Waffen SS headquarters, the KZ Inspectorate was, confusingly, incorporated within it. In consequence the new force included *Totenkopf Wachsturmbanne* – KZ guard units formed from militarily non-employable members of the general SS after the transfer of Eicke's Death's Head units to the front. Himmler's characteristically imprecise nomenclature was to occasion a great deal of controversy after the war; we shall therefore restrict our use of the term 'Waffen SS' solely to the military formations of the *Schutzstaffeln*.

Their baptism of fire in the *Blitzkrieg* against Poland had been inordinately bloody – a fact duly noted by the 'senior service', Himmler was to complain a year later. 'After the Polish campaign the Wehrmacht said we had huge casualties because we were not trained for the job; after the French campaign they suppose we have not fought.' Though Waffen SS casualties in the West were proportionately lighter than in Poland, the underlying attitude had not changed. Thus when Eicke reported to his Wehrmacht superior, General Hoepner, that the SS *Totenkopf* division had carried out orders irrespective of losses, the latter commented 'This is the mentality of a butcher'.

Hopener spoke more truly than he knew. Transferring to the West the standard of barbarism which they had employed against Polish 'subhumanity', on 27 May 1940 *Totenkopf* men massacred a hundred men of the 2nd Royal Norfolks after their capture. (Private Pooley, the only prisoner not killed outright, had crawled out of the mound of corpses under cover of darkness and surrendered to another German unit; severely disabled, he was repatriated in 1943. No one in Britain would believe his story.)

In German eyes the Waffen SS had emerged from the war in the West like a breed of latter-day Siegfrieds. Whipped along by aggressive rage they stormed across the Low Countries and France with total disregard for casualties. The first Iron Cross of the entire campaign went to a soldier of the *Leibstandarte*, a unit whose divisional battle honours included Rotterdam and Boulogne.

Despite this added prestige, the Waffen SS remained strictly subordinate to the Wehrmacht – both in terms of command and of numbers. Hitler refused point-blank to amend a ruling under which the allocation of manpower to the fighting services devolved upon the General Officers commanding the Reich's various military districts. In October 1940 Himmler by-passed this limitation by extending SS recruitment to volunteers from Scandinavia, the Low Countries and France. It seemed an auspicious moment for enlisting 'reserves of blood of value to the struggle of the Nordic race' in a European anti-Communist force, because Russia had just annexed Finnish and Rumanian territory by force or threat of force.

Even so the European SS was more of a symbol than a real force capable of solving the Black Order's manpower problems. But a solution was at hand – thanks to Gottlob Berger, an ex-gym instructor in his forties who, after directing Henlein's Freikorps bullies in the Sudeten crisis of autumn 1938, had become head of the SS *Führungsamt* (Leadership Office).

The athletic, romantic Berger (he liked mountaineering and filming eagles and buzzards in flight) had a son-in-law who was leader of the German minority group in Rumania. It was this family link that inspired Berger's foolproof suggestion for overcoming the manpower deficiency of the Waffen SS: recruitment among the millions of *Volksdeutsche* whose residence outside the Reich rendered them ineligible for conscription by the Wehrmacht.

Berger's plan combined subtlety – Himmler could outmanœuvre the generals without being drawn into demarcation disputes over manpower – with the built-in ideological advantage that most Balkan Germans entertained a deep hatred for their Slav neighbours.

This point was amply illustrated by the *Volksdeutsche* Prinz Eugen division, who in the course of anti-partisan operations in Yugoslavia executed innumerable civilian hostages and perpetrated a series of massacres of entire village populations (for instance at Kosutica in August 1943).

Not that German-born Waffen SS men acted in a noticeably different manner. When, after their first winter setbacks in Southern Russia, advancing SS units discovered the mutilated corpses of six SS soldiers in the courtyard of the Taganrog OGPU (Soviet Secret Police) headquarters, *Leibstandarte* commander Sepp Dietrich ordered the massacre of four thousand Russian prisoners of war in a bloodbath lasting three days and nights.

Such barbarities did not prevent the Waffen SS performing prodigious feats of valour on the Eastern front. After Red Army units had infiltrated the rear of the Wehrmacht's Central Group, General Model ordered Obersturmbannführer Kumm of the SS regiment *Der Führer* to hold a line along the bend of the Volga in temperatures of well below zero, while the Ninth Army regrouped. Four weeks later Kumm personally reported to Model 'Mission accomplished'. Adding 'My regiment is drawn up outside', he pointed to thirty-five survivors out of an original complement of two thousand.

Locked in a pitiless struggle with the Red Army partisans, the weather, mud, vermin and disease, SS soldiers drew sustenance from both spiritual and material sources. Their greatest single source of spiritual strength lay in the fact that He who had made their honour synonymous with loyalty to Himself existed: 'And then we sat there,' wrote a combat-weary SS man at Vessoloye, 'on the clay floor and listened to the voice we love so dearly. All of us fastened eyes on the loudspeaker – as if he were standing there, the Führer. . . . Is there a finer reward after a day of battle than to hear him? Never!'

Though this diary entry carries absolute conviction, there were in fact other, equally fine, rewards awaiting the battle-stained Waffen SS man – as is attested by a note from the Chief SS Economic Administrator Oswald Pohl, headed 'Concerning the distribution of watches to members of the Waffen SS': 'Stored at Oranienburg concentration camp at present are 24,000 pocket watches, 5,000 fountain pens, 4,000 wrist watches, 3,000 alarm clocks and 80 stop-watches. These gifts are presented to the worthiest members of the division in your name.'

The sound of Hitler's voice and a gold watch taken from a Jew – these contrasting and yet complementary incentives indicate the poles of the spectrum of SS emotions; in between ranged fanaticism yoked to incontinence, self-denial laced with rapacity, rage fuelled by total non-feeling.

Despite their unique motivation the deeds of the Waffen SS for long barely stood out – in the world's awareness at any rate – from the global welter of violence, suffering and confusion. There was one exception, however: the punitive action against Lidice, a village near Prague, on 9 June 1942. Heydrich, the Reich protector of Bohemia and Moravia (since September 1941), had been assassinated in a Prague street by Czech patriots, said to have come from Lidice. In reprisal, the village was razed to the ground, all male inhabitants above the age of fifteen were shot, the women consigned to concentration camps and the children dragged off to Lebensborn homes (whence those unsuitable for Germanization were also despatched to KZs). This obliteration of a peaceful village received maximum exposure in the Nazi propaganda media so as to crush occupied Europe's will to resist.

Fearful retribution was also visited upon political suspects in Czechoslovakia and imprisoned Jews everywhere – as though a bloodbath (code-name 'Aktion Reinhardt') could expunge the fact that at the height of Nazi power Heydrich, the second highest leader of the SS, had fallen to a patriot's bullet. His corpse was taken for a final display at the Reich Chancellery. Here the funeral orator Hitler touched the heads of the two little Heydrich boys (whom Himmler was holding by the hand) and then the Berlin Philharmonic Orchestra intoned Wagner's Funeral March. In the black Valhalla to which Hitler had consigned him in his oration Heydrich was soon joined by another founding father of the SS. In February 1943 'Papa' Eicke, founder of the concentration camp system and subsequently commander of the Waffen SS *Totenkopf* division, was shot down by the Russians while on a reconnaissance flight over their lines.

Obergruppenführer Eicke, who a year earlier – at the Battle of Demjansk – had prevented a German *débâcle* of almost Stalingrad proportions, aroused such fanatical devotion among his men that a *Totenkopf* unit risked their lives to bring back his body from inside Russian-held terrain.

Before his death Eicke had on a number of occasions articulated a corporate SS suspicion that Wehrmacht commanders sent the Waffen SS to the most exposed sectors of the front in order to decimate the force by ensuring inevitable heavy losses.

Whatever the motive, SS divisions were in fact thrown into some of the most crucial battles of the Eastern Front. The resulting casualty rate – coupled with the natural propensities of SS men – accounted for Waffen SS cases outnumbering all others on the weekly (Oberkommando der Wehrmacht, or Armed Forces High Command) reports of grave misdemeanours (rape, etc.) in the armed forces, and this despite an average Wehrmacht : Waffen SS ratio of ten to one.

The early growth of the Waffen SS had been steady – one division in the Polish campaign, two in the French – and even the subsequent expansion (creation of the European SS and, more importantly, *Volksdeutsche* recruitment) had been kept within bounds acceptable to the Wehrmacht. In the winter of 1942–3 three newly armoured SS divisions were grouped into an army corps under Paul Hausser, who had won his spurs as a tank commander in 1940. Shortly afterwards the great tank battle of Kharkov gave Hausser the opportunity for achieving a unique distinction: he became (in March 1943) the last German general of the Second World War to win a victory in the East.

This notable feat invalidated all Wehrmacht objections to the expansion of the Waffen SS and made Hitler authorize the immediate enlargement of the force. A second SS armoured corps was formed under Sepp Dietrich, followed (in the winter of 1943–4) by a third under Felix Steiner – a former Reichswehr officer who had switched to the *Verfügungstruppe* because the military establishment frowned on his unconventional ideas.

But this upgrading of the Waffen SS in size and importance occurred only after the tide of battle had irreversibly turned. There had been too long a delay in equipping the Waffen SS with heavy armour – besides which a third of its cadre divisions lay buried in Russia by the end of 1943.

These losses were compounded with the deteriorating quality of the new intake into the force. The volunteers who had, up to the end of 1942, sufficed to meet all SS manpower requirements had to be supplanted by conscripts, some of whom – influenced by their families or priests – showed a marked aversion to joining.

At a time when the Reich had already forfeited victory, but seemed as yet insulated from defeat, some SS leaders began to show an unwonted degree of ideological independence. Strenuously casting round for a political solution to military stalemate – or worse – Waffen SS General Steiner, the former *Schwarze Korps* editor d'Alquen, who had become head of the Wehrmacht's propaganda company, and others suggested a drastic modification of Nazi policy towards the Russians.

Desperate situations call for desperate remedies. The SS ethos was the quintessence of Nazi racism; to guide SS soldiers in the East, Gottlob Berger's office in 1941 published an instructional pamphlet 'The Subhuman', which called the peoples of the Soviet Union 'the afterbirth of humanity existing on a lower level spiritually than animals'.

Now General Steiner told Himmler that the war could only be won by conceding sovereignty to national groups in occupied Russia, and SD reports from the Ukraine pointedly attributed increases in partisan activity to the repression practised by Gauleiter Koch. The *Schwarze Korps* and d'Alquen's Wehrmacht propagandists undertook a public relations operation on behalf of General Vlassov – the renegade former Red Army commander heading a Nazi-sponsored force of released Russian prisoners of war – with the object of elevating him to the figurehead of a semi-sovereign Russian state under German tutelage.

D'Alquen's maverick public relations exercise, SD exposures of Koch's misrule, Steiner's reappraisal of nationality problems – none of this helped. Although late in the war Himmler modified his own racial conceptions to the extent of setting up the Russian SS Kaminski

Brigade, Hitler remained obdurate. On the Führer's scale of sub-humanity, Slavdom ranked but one degree above Gypsies and Jews. While d'Alquen concocted the nickname 'hero-liberator' for the pathetic Vlassov, Hitler held fast to his vision of Slavs as helots fit only to serve their German masters and thus frustrated the belated attempt by a handful of high-ranking members of the SS to wriggle out of a racist straitjacket of their own making.

5

The Final Solution

WHATEVER THE CONSEQUENCES OF HITLER'S SLAVOPHOBIA, ideologically it took second place to anti-Semitism. War to the death against the Jews was in fact the irreducible kernel of the Nazi creed – and in this war the SS manned the front line with frenzied dedication.

The Jews of the Reich had endured mounting persecution since 1933, to which growing numbers reacted by emigration. In a Reichstag speech on 30 January 1939 Hitler had openly avowed his intentions of genocide – 'a future war will see the destruction of the Jewish race in Europe' – but neither world opinion nor world Jewry could at that point in time fathom the awesome implications of his statement.

The coming of war and German conquests added new dimensions of scale and horror to the plight of the Jews. All emigration routes were blocked while the wartime black-out on communications freed Hitler from any vestigial inhibitions about implementing the so-called 'Final Solution'.

In September 1939 the head offices of the Gestapo, the SD and the Kriminalpolizei were merged into the *Reichssicherheitshauptamt* (RSHA or Reich Security Main Office) – keystone of an edifice of terror that soon spanned a continent. Heydrich became first head of the RSHA; his most important subordinate was Untersturmführer Adolf Eichmann, who in January 1940 took charge of the Jewish Department, the notorious subsection IV B 4, which functioned at a house in Berlin's select Kurfürstenstrasse crammed with filing cabinets, teleprinters and other office equipment.

At this very time the expulsion of Jews from the German-incorporated areas of Poland into rump-Poland (the so-called *Gouvernement-Général*) was taking a huge toll of lives through cold, hunger and disease. The winter clearance of the Warthegau was not the only foretaste of things to come for Polish Jewry: ever since their arrival in the country SS and police units had undertaken sporadic mass-shootings and burnings of synagogues.

Above the gates of Auschwitz: 'Work makes you free'

Concentration camp Dachau. The inscription states: 'There is only one road to freedom. Its milestones are obedience, industry, honesty, order, cleanliness, sobriety, truthfulness, readiness to sacrifice and love of country'

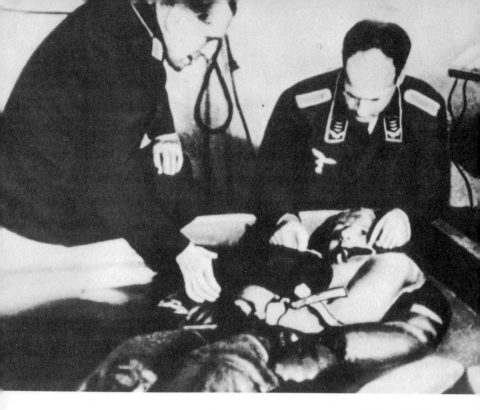

KZ medical
'research'. A
super-cooling
experiment
during which
Dr. Rascher
immersed
Dachau inmates
in freezing water
for up to three
hours (1942)

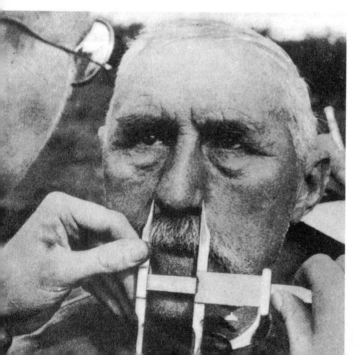

SS race research

Inmates working in the quarry at Mauthausen KZ (1938)

'Celebrating' the recapture of an escaped concentration camp inmate

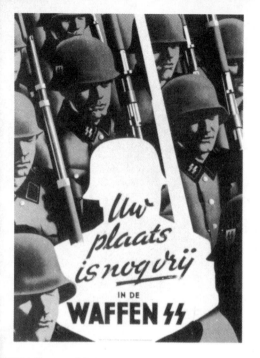

Dutch recruiting poster for the
Waffen SS

Norwegian recruiting poster for the
Waffen SS

Title page of the SS periodical
'*Die Schutzstaffel*'

Himmler, Heydrich and other SS high-ups in the crypt of the medieval
Quedlinburg – the alleged burial place of Henry the Fowler

Pour encourager les autres. The inscription on the white board states (in Russian): 'I was a partisan'

Central Front 1943. Russian women take the mutilated remains of their menfolk back to their village for burial

'SS home guard Danzig' at the outbreak of the Second World War

Members of the Hitler jugend division of the Waffen SS in Normandy

SS leaders at war: Sepp Dietrich
and Himmler on the Polish front
(1939)

General Paul Hauser,
father of the Waffen SS

'Papa' Eicke, father of
the KZ system, walking
pipe in mouth after the
battle of Demjansk
(1942)

The first winter of the war also saw the deportation of Jews from south-west Germany to camps in unoccupied France – in pursuance of Eichmann's nebulous 'Madagascar scheme' for turning the French island colony in the Indian Ocean into a Jewish reservation. Huge *Judenreservate* were created during 1940-1, when Poland's three million Jews were inexorably herded into a few unimaginably overcrowded ghettoes – in Warsaw, Cracow, Lodz, Bialystock. 'Natural wastage' had already eliminated half a million ghetto dwellers before Hitler's final escalation of the war, the attack on Russia, created the setting for the climax of the Jewish catastrophe. Three months before Operation Barbarossa, the Führer instructed Himmler – in the notorious 'Commissars' Order' – to set up *Einsatzgruppen* (killer units) for the 'ruthless liquidation of all Bolshevik agitators, partisans, saboteurs and Jews found behind the Russian lines'.

Though Jews figured last in this order they provided the main quarry for the three-thousand-strong, highly mobile *Einsatz* commandos who scoured the vast area between the Gulf of Finland and the Black Sea on the heels of the advancing Wehrmacht. The Baltic States, White Russia and the Ukraine were areas of dense Jewish settlement; moreover, the lightning German advances during 1941 overran communities which Soviet censorship had – particularly since the Russo-German Pact of August 1939 – long kept in ignorance of the fate of their fellow-Jews under Nazi rule.

In these circumstances the tasks of the *Einsatzgruppen* were reduced to simple logistics: the round-up of the Jews in a village or town square, their transport to a secluded site traversed by a deep ditch, and, spaced correctly, their lining-up in the executioners' gun-sights. The ideal, rationalized solution was one whereby successive line-ups neatly produced layer upon layer of bodies in the ditch, which was then covered over with earth.

This economy of effort, though influenced by the smallness of the 'force', basically reflected the built-in economic orientation of the Nazi machinery of death: before stepping to the edge of the mass grave, victims had to undress and place their clothes, shoes, valuables and other belongings in separate files for subsequent – rational – utilization.

In all, the *Einsatzgruppen* liquidated an estimated 1,300,000 Jews, which, considering the 1 : 430 ratio of hunters to hunted, speaks volumes for their tireless dedication and efficiency. This score remains staggering even after allowances are made for the supporting role of

German soldiers or local volunteers – no less than for the competitive spirit which made *Einsatz* group commanders inflate their death tallies to outpace colleagues and impress superiors at RSHA, Berlin. What manner of men were these latter-day Genghis Khans with a weakness for 'adjusting' the scorebook? Surprisingly enough few of them could be classified as outright thugs or psychopaths. Walter Stahlecker, leader of *Einsatzgruppe* A, which scored a 'first' by reporting Estonia clear of Jews in record time, had come straight from a top administrative post – Head of Foreign Intelligence – at the Reich Security Main Office. Dr Stahlecker was an intellectual of sorts – as was Otto Ohlendorf, his opposite number, both as leader of *Einsatzgruppe* D (Ukraine and Crimea) and as sometime Head of Internal Intelligence at the Reich Security Main Office.

University graduates were also strongly in evidence among middle-ranking *Einsatzgruppe* officers. Standartenführer Paul Blobel, responsible for the horrifying massacre of thirty thousand Jews at Babi Yar near Kiev, was an architect laid low by drink. Blobel's colleague, Bieberstein, was a theology graduate. When the Nuremberg judge asked this unfrocked ex-pastor in 1947 if it had ever occurred to him to offer spiritual comfort to his victims, Bieberstein replied, 'They were Bolsheviks – one should not cast pearls before swine. If I tell atheists the word of God I run the risk that they'll turn ironic. These things are too sacred for me to risk in such situations.'

At Nuremberg Blobel exuded self-pity – an attitude which, though superficially at odds with the prescribed SS image, could be dressed up as an expression of the Germans' much-vaunted capacity for inwardness. 'Human life was not as valuable to them, i.e. to the Russians and Jews, as to us. Our men who took part in these executions suffered more than those who had to be shot.'

The conscientious junior officer's concern for the well-being of his subordinates also shone through the Nuremberg reminiscences of another of the accused: 'In the mornings I would take my men to the lakeside for sports and in the evenings we had sing-songs around the camp fire.'

The only point on which the *Einsatzgruppen* officers in the dock significantly disagreed concerned the methodology of murder. Some considered execution by shooting 'more honourable' than by gas, while others, such as Bieberstein, expressed a preference for gassing as 'more pleasant for both parties concerned'.

Death by gassing, to which the Eastern *Einsatz* commandos had only resorted intermittently, became from Winter 1941–2 standard practice in the *Judenreservate* of the *Gouvernement-Général*. At Chelmo in Poland a pilot gas-chamber plant was already operational some weeks before the historic Wannsee Conference on the Final Solution (January 1942). This conference, chaired by Heydrich with Eichmann taking the minutes and attended by RSHA dignitaries and State Secretaries from a dozen Ministries, devised the master plan for the extermination of the Jews throughout the continent.

Within the next few months four gas-chamber complexes – Belcez, Sobibor, Majdanek and Treblinka – sprang up in the Lublin region, a vast reception area for deported Jews administered by Gruppenführer Odilo Globocnik. Globocnik's aide in charge of the actual death camp organization was Christian Wirth, who had supervised the euthanasia campaign. Like all who had risen high in the SS *Apparat*, Wirth was surrounded by powerful enemies, some of whom – unfortunately for him – were present at Belcez one August day on 1942 when the following scene occurred:

'At 7.20 a.m. a train arrived from Lemberg with 45 wagons holding more than 6,000 people. Of these 1,450 were already dead on arrival. Behind the small barbed-wire windows, children, young ones, frightened to death, women and men. As the train drew in 200 Ukrainians detailed for the task tore open the doors and laying about them with their leather whips drove the Jews out of the cars. Instructions boomed from a loudspeaker ordering them to remove all clothing, artificial limbs and spectacles. Using small pieces of string handed out by a little Jewish boy they were to tie their shoes together. All valuables and money were to be handed in at the valuables counter but no voucher or receipt was given. Women and girls were to have their hair cut off in the hairdresser's hut.

'At the corner stood a burly SS man with a loud, priest-like voice. "Nothing terrible is going to happen to you. All you have to do is to breathe in deeply. That strengthens the lungs. Inhaling is a means of preventing infectious diseases." They asked what was going to happen to them. "The men will have to work building houses and roads. But the women won't be obliged to do so; they'll do housework or help in the kitchen." For some this was a last small ray of hope, enough to carry them, unresisting, as far as the chambers of death. Most of them knew the truth. The odour told them what their fate was to be. They walked up a small flight of steps and into the death chambers, most of them without a word, thrust forward by those behind them.

'Inside the chambers SS men were crushing the people together. "Fill them up well," Wirth had ordered, "700 or 800 of them to every 270 square feet." Now the doors were closed. Meanwhile the rest of the people from the train stood waiting, naked.

'An SS sergeant, the driver of the diesel truck whose exhaust gases were to be used, was making great efforts to get the engine running, but it refused to start. Fifty minutes, seventy minutes ticked away but the diesel would not work. Inside the gas chamber the people could be heard weeping. Furious at the delay Wirth lashed out with his whip at the Ukrainian assisting the SS sergeant.

'It was 2 hours and 49 minutes before the diesel started. At the end of another 32 minutes all were dead. Some Jewish workers on the far side opened the wooden doors. Inside the people were still standing erect like pillars of basalt, since there had not been an inch of space for them to fall in or even lean. The bodies were tossed out, blue, wet with sweat and urine, the legs soiled with faeces and menstrual blood. A couple of dozen workers checked the mouths of the dead, which they tore open with iron hooks. Other workers inspected anus and genital organs in search of money, diamonds, gold, dentists moved around hammering out gold teeth, bridges and crowns. In the midst of them stood Hauptsturmführer Wirth, in his element.'

But Wirth was not to stand in the middle much longer. During the 2 hours 49 minutes of lost killing time an internal SS controversy about the relative merits of carbon monoxide and *Zyklon B* (prussic acid) as asphyxiating agents had achieved resolution. This technical controversy marked, as frequently happens, a personal power-struggle – so that when, as a result of the diesel failure at Belcez, *Zyklon B* replaced carbon monoxide in all camps, and Wirth went down before Hauptsturmführer Karl Fritzsch, spokesman for the prussic acid lobby.

Fritzsch was on the staff of Auschwitz, the camp SS personnel dubbed – with characteristic self-pity – *anus mundi*. (Here the still-living envied the dead: hunger-crazed Russian prisoners expended their last ounce of strength hoisting themselves on to the carts which every evening conveyed the corpses of the day's dead to the burning pit.)

Auschwitz dominated the death-camp network both in size – four crematoria comprising forty-six ovens could handle five hundred corpses per hour, and still required supplementing by huge open incineration pits – and in diversity. Besides gas chambers and crematoria the camp accommodated (on fifteen square miles between the rivers Vistula and Sola) a huge industrial complex of arms workshops, chemical factories, synthetic petrol and rubber works, railway repair shops, quarries, forestry and farm enterprises – all staffed by slave labour.

Despite all this varied industry, its chief product was death: a commodity in which Auschwitz averaged an annual output of over a million throughout the three years of its existence.

On arrival at the camp whose gates bore the inscription *Arbeit Macht Frei* (Work Makes You Free), prisoners underwent selection either for instant despatch to the gas chambers or for more protracted extermination through work. During the few months (at most) which, except in the case of specially needed craftsmen, separated a worker's arrival from his final selection, he subsisted in a state of inconceivable degradation and helplessness. The trauma of being thrust into this inferno reduced him overnight from human individuality to animal reflexes; nameless, his identity diminished to the number tattooed on the right forearm, he became a speck of dust which existed for only so long as one of the SS men or *Kapos* (trusties) did not flick it off.

Slave labour on starvation rations was punctuated by endless rollcalls, debilitating parodies of military routine – prisoners were drilled for hours to take their caps off before SS men who had to be passed at the double at a distance of six paces with arms stiff and held tightly to the body – and by savage punishment.

Ex-police commissar Wilhelm Boger, the head of the camp's escape department, carried out his investigations by means of the 'Boger swing'. Two tables stood about three feet apart. The victim was made to sit down on the floor and fold his hands in front of his bent knees. Then his wrists were handcuffed, a heavy rod inserted between his elbows and knees, and the ends of the rods put on the tables. Thus he swung helplessly between the tables. The victim was then hit with a bullwhip on his backside and the soles of his feet so that he would turn an almost complete somersault. When his cries became too loud, a gas mask was pulled over his face; this was removed from time to time to see if he was ready to 'confess' or had lost consciousness.

The deputy camp commandant, Robert Mulka, a former businessman, liked to indulge in rabbit hunts: prisoners had their caps knocked off and when they stopped to pick them up they were shot – 'killed while trying to escape'.

Auschwitz's medical officer Dr Mengele demonstrated a less primitive sense of humour. On Yom Kippur (Day of Atonement) two thousand Jewish boys assembled on the camp's football ground and were made to pass under a plank nailed to the goalposts; all those whose heads did not touch the plank had to go to one side, and were subsequently gassed. (On the Day of Atonement the Jews recite a prayer describing the Lord as a shepherd who passes his flock under a rod.)

Every camp produced variations on the SS officers' favourite theme of mocking the Jewish religion in the very act of wiping it out. The commandant of Treblinka appointed a 'shitmaster' who, attired in rabbinical garb and armed with alarm-clock and whip, had to enforce time-limits among the dysentry-afflicted users of the camp latrines.

At Belcez the doors of the gas chamber were draped in synagogue curtains bearing the Hebrew inscription, 'This is the gate of the Lord through which the righteous shall enter'; and the way into the death compound from the guards' quarters was signposted 'Entrance to the Jewish State'.

At Auschwitz the guards whiled away their off-duty hours with sport naively untinged by religious allusions. They would order prisoners to put mice inside their trousers (which were tightly bound below) and to stand to motionless attention – on pain of being whipped – with the rodents crawling over their bodies. Prisoners had bottles placed on their heads and shot off; they were made to walk planks seven metres off the ground – an 'enemy parachutist' (anyone who fell off) received twenty-five lashes – or were savaged by huge dogs who on the order of 'Man, attack dog' literally tore their victims to pieces.

But it would be wrong to speak of all SS camp personnel as thorough-going embodiments of evil. One of the medical officers at Auschwitz, responsible for 'selecting' thousands, saved the life of a woman doctor who had attended the same university as himself and pretended to remember him as an habitué of the local student tavern.

When Sturmbannführer Höfle, an aide of Globocnik's with two hundred thousand deportations to his credit, lost a daughter in a diphtheria epidemic he sobbed at the grave: 'This is the punishment of heaven for all my misdeeds.'

Ohlendorf felt a need for dressing up the massacres perpetrated by his *Einsatzgruppe* D as military executions, and Himmler himself was taken ill watching a mass-shooting at Minsk in 1942 – whereupon Gruppenführer Wolff remarked to his escorts: 'Let him just see what he demands of others.'

Höfle's and Wolff's graveside *cris-de-cœur* showed the perversion of vestigial stirrings of conscience into self-pitying cliché – a feeling of being hard done by alternated with the euphoria of violence as a stock SS emotion. Thus Gendarmeriemeister Fritz Jacob complained bitterly at having to exterminate Jews while enduring separation from his family.

When Globocnik had 'dissolved' all the camps under his jurisdiction by late 1943, he querulously reminded Himmler of the iron crosses promised for 'this hard work' – it was unfair that the 'smaller Warsaw enterprise' (i.e., the crushing, in April 1943, of the heroic Ghetto rising by Waffen SS Brigadeführer Jürgen Stroop) should have brought Stroop's men greater rewards for less effort.

Globocnik's dissolution of the Lublin camp complex signified that another internal SS controversy – between advocates of the extermination of the Jews and advocates of their employment as slave labour – had been concluded; in the Jewish as in the Russian question, Nazi race dogma blotted out all considerations of German national self-interest.

The SS department most affected by this decision was Oswald Phol's *Wirtschafts und Verwaltungs Hauptamt* (WVHA, or Economic Administration Main Office). The ex-naval paymaster Pohl had been Himmler's economic overlord ever since the Reichsführer's decision to found an economic empire on concentration-camp labour in 1938. Under Pohl's aegis SS enterprises concerned with arms production, textile and leather manufacture, food processing and the distilling of non-alcoholic beverages had grown by the middle of the war to reach an annual turnover of fifty million Reichsmark.

The SS industry to show the fastest growth rate was armaments. Its director, Dr Hans Kammler, a technocrat of rambling ambition, also masterminded the construction of gas chambers, barracks, hangars and underground factories; in addition Kammler built launching sites for flying bombs and V2 rockets – top priority tasks for which he requisitioned a labour force of 175,000 prisoners of war and KZ inmates in 1942.

At this stage of the war Pohl's slave-driving senior executives became concerned about concentration camp labour being a diminishing asset: during December 1942 alone an overall KZ population increase (through continent-wide raids and manhunts) of 136,000 had to be offset against a 'natural' wastage rate of 70,000. Something clearly had to be done; the WVHA accordingly forbade the ill-treatment of KZ labourers and limited their working day to eleven hours.

To squeeze the last reserves of strength (and profitability) out of the surviving quarter of Polish Jewry, Pohl's men early in 1943 set up *Ostindustrie GmbH*, but as all its 'employees' were liquidated within that year the firm eventually went into liquidation, too.

Even then the supply of labour for the slave empire of the *Schutzstaffeln* did not dry up. One source of replenishment was the millions of foreign conscript workers in the Reich. By an arrangement between Himmler and Justice Minister Thierack of 1942, any foreign worker guilty of absenteeism, rationing offences or contact with German women was automatically sent to a concentration camp. During the first half of 1943 alone 200,000 suffered this form of punishment; a year later in 1944 Armament Minister Speer complained to Hitler that the SS were still bagging his labour force at the rate of 30–40,000 a month.

In the final twelve months of the war Pohl's slave-labour army numbered 600,000; 250,000 toiled in privately-owned arms factories (such as Krupps'), 170,000 in state-run 'Speer enterprises', 130,000 in agriculture and service industries and the remainder on construction sites.

Though by this time the situation of the Reich was growing increasingly abnormal, certain normal laws still applied – such as the ineluctable law of supply and demand. As shortages placed labour at a premium, SS 'entrepreneurs' able to supply the market with this scarce commodity – of whatever quality – stood to make a sizeable profit. The exact amount of profit involved, the ratio of yield to investment, emerges from this statement prepared by the cost-accounting department of the WVHA:

'The hiring out of concentration camp inmates to industrial enterprises yields an average daily return of 6 to 8 marks from which 70 pfennigs must be deducted for food and clothing. Assuming a camp inmate's life expectancy of 9 months we multiply this sum by 270; the total is 1,431 marks. This profit can be increased by rational utilization of the corpse, i.e. by means of gold fillings, clothing, valuables, etc., but on the other hand every corpse represents a loss of two marks which is the cost of cremation.'

In theory this profit accrued to the Reich; in practice it frequently went to one of the Reichsführer's minions, such as the commandant at Buchenwald, Hermann Pister, who amassed a personal fortune by supplying Ruhr industrialists with KZ labour. When negotiating with

Russian Jews begging for food (1941)

Access bridge to the Lodz ghetto (1941)

Auschwitz: arrival

Auschwitz: the ovens

Auschwitz: what remained

Belsen, April 1945. On British instructions camp guards bury their victims in mass graves

Krupp, Mannesmann, and the rest, Oberführer Pister could almost claim to be a fellow-tycoon since, in addition to his KZ post, he held lucrative directorships in the SS arms manufacturing company, the SS construction company and so forth.

Pister, though, still fell short of his predecessor, Buchenwald Lagerkommandant Koch who, after the *Kristallnacht* round-up of thousands of Jews in November 1938, had diverted vast wealth 'forfeit to the Reich' into his own pockets. Himmler, who held very strong views on the subject of corruption – though not totally averse to taking financial advantage of his position, he would deduct the cost of 'official' petrol used on family outings from his personal salary, told SS leaders at Posen in October 1943, 'We have taken the Jews' riches away from them; whoever touches a single Reichsmark forfeits his life.'

Himmler's draconian avowal rang both true and false. Harsh discipline and meagre pay invested the SS with an aura of austerity, but this was a smokescreen behind which Nazism – aptly defined as 'an appeal to the inner *Schweinehund* inside every German' by the Social Democrat leader Kurt Schuhmacher – acted as a goad to every base instinct.

6

Collapse of the Third Reich

CORRUPT CONDUCT WITHIN THE 'SCHUTZSTAFFELN' ELICITED retribution in a highly selective manner. Each Nazi institution was a hierarchy in which punishment depended on the offender's place in the pecking order; thus after an investigation of the Warsaw-based Waffen SS Cavalry Division on charges of currency fraud and deals in confiscated Jewish property, two junior officers were executed while their heavily implicated commander Hermann Fegelein, show-jumper, founder of the (aristocratic) Reiter SS and Hitler's 'brother-in-law' – through his marriage to Gretel Braun – got off scot-free.

By the same token Koch's Buchenwald bonanza hinged on Eicke and Pohl, whose connivance the affluent Lagerkommandant purchased by regular gifts of 10,000 Reichsmark. Though the tax office responsible for Buchenwald, and the regional SS and Police leader Prince Waldeck-Pyrmont (a bitter adversary of Koch's), repeatedly pressed for an investigation of the camp's tangled finances, Koch's Midas touch even survived the front-line posting of chief KZ administrator Eicke in 1941. Some time later Himmler did, however, sanction an inquiry – either out of revived puritanical zeal or because he felt the need to curb his overmighty subject Pohl.

The SS investigator Dr Morgen encountered endless evasion – climaxed by Koch's evasive action in getting transferred to the Lublin camp command before Dr Morgen had even started on the case. At Lublin, where the new commandant relied on Globocnik's powerful protection, his corrupt rule soon resulted in a mass escape attempt after which – to deprive Dr Morgen of potential prosecution witnesses – Koch had thousands of prisoners slaughtered.

Nonetheless, particularly on account of the attempted mass breakout, Koch was eventually judicially executed – an extremely unusual ending to a corrupt (in the Nazi sense) SS career. Thus Rudolf Höss, the ex-Freikorps murderer who became first Lagerkommandant of Auschwitz, was charged with misappropriating gold from teeth in 1943; found 'guilty', he had to exchange his Auschwitz command for the

Deputy Inspectorate of concentration camps – a higher post with fewer bonuses! Promotion as a result of blatant misconduct – a paradigm of SS judicial processes. Oskar Dirlewanger, a convicted child-rapist and head of a Waffen SS *Sonderkommando* staffed by discharged convicts, came to Dr Morgen's attention through reports of widespread looting and racketeering in the Cracow ghetto. When applying for a warrant for his arrest, the investigator discovered that Dirlewanger – whose officers' mess diversions included injecting Jewish girls with strychnine and watching their death agonies – was not subject to the jurisdiction of the regional SS and Police leader but to that of Gottlob Berger at SS Main Office, Berlin.

On receiving Dr Morgen's application Berger posted Dirlewanger to anti-partisan duties in White Russia and promoted him to Oberführer *en route*.

The *affaires* Koch, Höss and Dirlewanger are illustrations of the way in which inter-departmental rivalries – regional SS and Police leader versus Lagerkommandant, Waffen SS command versus regional SS and Police leader – determined SS judicial processes. Both within the Black Order and the Nazi state as a whole the combating of corruption was little more than a function of the rivalry between competing power cliques.

The first prerequisite for the cleaning-up of corruption is a visible distinction between right and wrong, which was totally absent from Nazi society. In the Third Reich it could happen that the medical officer of a concentration camp obtained a doctorate at the University of Freiburg on the strength of a dissertation written for him – in exchange for survival rations – by two Buchenwald inmates. More crucially, in the Third Reich it was possible for three hundred and fifty trained doctors (one in every three hundred of the medical profession) to take part in medical KZ experiments dressed up as research. Their experiments covered a wide spectrum of 'medical science' and inflicted indescribably agonizing deaths on countless camp inmates.

Research in sterilization techniques involved exposure to large doses of X-rays, straightforward castration, sterilization with drugs, and the injection of inflammatory liquid into the uterus. Other experiments entailed drinking sea-water, infection with gas, gangrenous wounds, bone transplants, exposure to phosgene and mustard gas, the artificial inducing of phlegmon, and so forth.

At KZ Neuengamme Dr Heisskeyer injected Jewish children with tuberculosis bacilli and watched their deaths. At KZ Dachau Dr Rascher conducted super-cooling experiments – for the alleged benefit of pilots forced to bale out into the sea – in which prisoners were immersed in near-freezing water for lengthy periods. Himmler, the dabbler in homeopathy, had picked up some old wives' tale according to which after sea-rescues the wives of North Sea fishermen took their half-frozen husbands to bed with them to warm them up; in consequence he ordered Dr Rascher to undertake resuscitation experiments with body heat and directed the women's KZ Ravensbruck to provide the doctor with four prostitutes as suppliers of 'animal warmth'. In his directive Himmler emphasized that the chosen four, who would come into physical contact with KZ inmates, must under no circumstances be German prostitutes.

The SS has often been described as a state within a state, but this is something of an over-simplification. The dynamics of power in the Third Reich are too complex for shorthand definitions, and unfortunately lack of space precludes further elaboration here. Perhaps both extremes can be avoided by an historical analogy, albeit tenuous, between the empires of Charlemagne and Hitler.

Both the First and the Third Reich were governed – under Holy Roman Emperor and Führer respectively – by powerful and mutually hostile feudatories: the Nazi counterparts of the Empire's warring dukes and margraves were the chiefs of the Party, the SS, the SA, the Propaganda Ministry, the Foreign Office, the Ministry of Eastern Territories, and the Labour Front. Combining abject deference to the Führer with venomous antipathy towards each other, Bormann, Himmler, Lutze, Goebbels, Ribbentrop, Rosenberg, Ley – not to mention the empire-builder *par excellence* Göring – were locked in civil strife with ever-changing fronts, allies, enemies and neutrals, and one constant factor: the struggle for power.

In this conflict Himmler managed to score over his rivals more often than they did over him. From his unassailable power base, he was ceaselessly encroaching on the sphere of competence of the Wehrmacht, the Ministry of the Interior, the Foreign Office, the Ministry of Eastern Territories and other institutions of the Nazi state. In August 1943 Himmler actually replaced Minister of the Interior Frick, whose purely nominal subordinate he had been since 1937.

The Himmler–Ribbentrop feud went back nearly as long and had been highlighted by SS forays into foreign affairs which ran counter to official Reich policy. Thus in Rumania in 1940 the Reich exerted pressure to install Marshal Antonescu as head of a pro-German administration while the SD produced a rival candidate: the Iron Guard leader Horia Sima. After Antonescu's assumption of power (with the aid of German troops who entered the country) the SD still supported an attempted Iron Guard coup – but to no avail. The discomfiture of the *Schutzstaffeln* was compounded by Ribbentrop's appointment of a whole batch of SA dignitaries as Reich ambassadors to Germany's Balkan satellites, where these survivors of the Röhm Putsch exercised vice-regal powers.

Not long afterwards the chance of a counter-stroke presented itself to the Black Order when Dr Luther, a departmental head at the Foreign Office, circulated among interested parties in Berlin a confidential memorandum about Ribbentrop's mental incapacity. Himmler, however, did not forward this document to Hitler since he was reluctant to provoke a showdown with Ribbentrop so soon after the 'Sima Affair'. More importantly, with Nazi victories rapidly reducing the area of Europe which was not German – and with it the scope for foreign policy-making – he may well have decided to concede to Ribbentrop the monopoly of an ever-shrinking field.

Henceforth Himmler concentrated on building up his power in Nazi-occupied Europe where, though up to 1943 heads of Army Groups outranked SS commanders on every front, in all rear areas the military were subordinate to the regional SS and Police leaders. Apart from exercising vast police powers, the SS contrived to infiltrate steadily into the administration of the occupied territories. In Poland they coerced Governor Hans Frank (an inveterate enemy of Himmler's) into appointing Higher SS and Police leader Krüger as his Secretary of State by the simple expedient of confronting him with evidence of his personal corruption unearthed by one of Dr Morgen's colleagues. In occupied Russia they gained additional leverage when the Reich Minister for Eastern Territories, Rosenberg, felt driven to enlist Gottlob Berger's aid against his own over-mighty subject, the uniquely refractory Reichskommissar Koch of the Ukraine.

But in the Nazi feudatories' war of all against all, fortune – or Hitler's countenance – hardly ever smiled on one of the belligerents consistently. While Himmler was enlarging his stake in the political administration of occupied Europe he met with a reverse in the economic sphere: his one-time accomplice (of Röhm Putsch days) Göring set up the *Haupttreuhandstelle Ost* (or Eastern Trustee Authority), which snatched up all confiscated industrial property in Poland and Russia.

At the height of the war Viktor Lutze, Röhm's colourless successor as SA Chief of Staff, joined Governor Hans Frank in an anti-Himmler *fronde* of considerable potential – Frau Lutze was related to the Wehrmacht Commander-in-Chief von Brauchitsch – but this threat evaporated when the stormtroop chief died soon afterwards in a car accident.

These intrigues and power struggles at Hitler's court had their counterpart within the narrower compass of the SS establishment. Although Himmler maintained no court in the accepted sense of the term, certain members of his immediate entourage had readier access to – and correspondingly greater influence over – the Reichsführer than senior officers outranking them. The key figure of this inner circle was Standartenführer Rudolf Brandt, the assiduous male typist promoted to Principal Aide, whose intercession was indispensable to anyone seeking audience with the Reichsführer. Less centrally placed was Dr Korherr, an academic who doubled as SS statistician and as Himmler's 'private eye' into the affairs of his top brass – an extramural activity which earned Korherr a nasty beating-up and eventual relegation to a provincial backwater. There was also the Finnish 'doctor' Felix Kersten, who owed his licence as political jester, and his ability to influence Himmler towards rare acts of mercy, to his skill in alleviating his exalted patient's chronic stomach cramps.

The death of Heydrich in June 1942 had left a vacuum at the apex of the SS power structure and Himmler prevaricated for eight months before filling it. The short list for the succession comprised three names: Dr Stuckart, Ernst Kaltenbrunner and Max Schellenberg, the head of SD Foreign Intelligence (whose suggestions for contacts with the chief of US Intelligence, Alan Dulles, in Switzerland during mid-1942 had been vetoed by Himmler in the aftermath of the Sima affair and the Luther Memorandum). Dr Stuckart was *Staatssekretät* at the Ministry of the Interior and Obergruppenführer Kaltenbrunner was Higher SS and Police leader of Vienna.

The eventual choice of Kaltenbrunner as head of the RSHA was influenced by Himmler's calculation that, as a newcomer to the capital and its cabals, the Austrian would prove a more pliable instrument in his hands than the others. The term 'pliable' may seem singularly inappropriate when applied to this scarfaced thug, but in fact Kaltenbrunner throughout fell short of establishing his predecessor's ascendancy over the six powerful departmental heads of the RSHA, who included Oswald Pohl and Gestapo Chief Heinrich Müller. It was 'Gestapo-Müller' who in early 1944 issued the notorious 'cartridge directive' under which Soviet prisoners of war who had helped to identify captured political commissars for purposes of liquidation were themselves executed as *Geheimnisträger* ('bearers of secrets'). This blood purge was soon extended to all Russian prisoners charged with attempting escape, refusing work or inciting disaffection.

Müller's decimation of the Russian camp population occurred at the same time as the extension of the Final Solution to Hungary's three-quarters of a million Jews. Diverting badly needed military rolling stock, a small staff of experts from department IV B 4 of the RSHA headed by Obersturmbannführer Eichmann – and assisted by Hungarian officials and Fascists of the Arrow Cross Party – in three short months effected the round-up and deportation of close on half a million to the gas chambers of Auschwitz.

By summer the greater part of Hungary was *judenrein* (cleared of Jews); but with the Allies in Normandy and Germany's fortunes declining, the Hungarian head of state Admiral Horthy stealthily prepared to stop the deportations and take his country out of the war. To foil this move a Waffen SS unit under Otto Skorzeny (who had snatched Mussolini from Allied captivity in a daring airborne coup a year earlier) was despatched to Budapest, where Horthy was abducted and taken back to the Reich as a prisoner; his Arrow Cross successors in government kept Hungary in the war and continued the deportations of the Jews.

The overthrow of Horthy was one of a series of Waffen SS triumphs gained in the rear of the fighting front during the closing stages of the war.

In August the distant approach of the Russians had triggered off a mass uprising in Warsaw. German forces in the Polish capital were headed by Gruppenführer von dem Bach-Zelewski, who disposed of police and Waffen SS contingents stiffened with Dirlewanger's criminal rabble and the Pole-hating Russian Kaminski Brigade. As the Red Army regrouped beyond the Vistula, Warsaw became engulfed in a Walpurgisnacht of death, fire and looting. The atrocities perpetrated by the *Sonderkommando* Dirlewanger were such that they caused the Wehrmacht Chief of Staff, General Guderian, to petition Hitler for redress, while Kaminski's conduct reputedly caused Bach-Zelewski to have him liquidated shortly after the crushing of the Warsaw revolt in October 1944.

Since besides Hungary and Poland the *Schutzstaffeln*'s battle honours

included Slovakia, where Obergruppenführer Gottlob Berger had
established the peace of the graveyard after an autumn uprising, the SS
star was now very much in the ascendant in the darkening sky of the
Third Reich.

Every passing month brought an accretion of Hitler's power. After
the failure of the July Plot, he supplanted General Fromm as Commander of the Replacement Army. He then took overall charge of the
V-weapons programme, and in October he assumed virtual command of the *Volksturm*, an emergency militia of German males between
sixteen and sixty (whose ideological training, however, remained
Bormann's responsibility).

What amounted to the investiture of an heir-apparent occurred on
9 November 1944: Himmler addressed the Munich Old Guard reunion
in place of the grateful Hitler – an unprecedented departure from
hallowed Party routine.

This political accolade was followed by an ambiguous military prefer-
ment. At the prompting of Bormann, who wanted to discredit his
militarily inexperienced rival, Himmler received command of the Army
Group Upper Rhine at the onset of the last winter of the war.

Though the war now had barely half a year to run, the German
people, the Wehrmacht and, above all, the SS were by and large still
besotted with the Führer. The Black Order overwhelmingly remained
faithful – the more so because non-Germans in the Waffen SS (who
by early 1945 actually outnumbered Reich citizens) fought with the
desperation of self-acknowledged traitors to their own countries.

The Waffen SS as a whole continued to perform prodigious military
feats and even managed to repeat their horrendous performance at
Lidice. Klissura in Northern Greece, for example, Oradour and Tulle
in France, Putten in Holland and other towns elsewhere all shared the
fate of the Czech mining village after equally little provocation. Hand
in hand with the slaughter of helpless civilians went that of unarmed
enemy soldiers: Waffen SS massacred their American prisoners
at Malmedy and Canadian captives at Ancienne Abbaye in the
Ardennes.

While the SS soldiery thus steadily added to their reputation for
military prowess and bloody excesses, some SS generals began to
entertain doubts about the Führer's infallibility in strategic matters.
After D-Day, Sepp Dietrich demanded a free hand for field commanders in the event of a collapse of the front and both Hausser
(promoted from the Second SS Armoured Corps to command of the

Seventh Army) and his successor Obergruppenführer Bittrich concurred in their Army Group commander Rommel's bitter criticism of Hitler's war strategy.

Rommel, who had been convinced of the impossibility of German victory by the Normandy landings, was also privy to the Officers' Plot of 20 July 1944, the failure of which led to his subsequent suicide at the behest of the Gestapo.

July 20 saw the climax of various schemes against Hitler which had been hatched by military and civilian resistance circles at least since the outbreak of war. The leading civilian plotter (and Chancellor-Designate of Free Germany) was Carl Goerdeler, the Conservative ex-Mayor of Leipzig. Among Goerdeler's closest associates was the former Prussian Finance Minister Dr Popitz. Popitz had an acquaintance, the lawyer Dr Langbehn, who happened to live next door to Himmler at Dahlem, a suburb of Berlin.

Early in 1943 Popitz asked Langbehn to sound out Himmler about putting out peace-feelers to the West, and the lawyer eventually succeeded in arranging for Popitz to meet the Reichsführer. The Resistance man told Himmler he was the one sufficiently powerful leader in Germany to extricate the country from a war which could not be won and urged him to depose Hitler and initiate talks with the British and Americans. Himmler – who thanks to Schellenberg was familiar with this line of reasoning – adopted a non-committal, though interested, attitude; however, when in September 1943 the Gestapo decoded messages implicating Langbehn in links with the Allies, he broke off all contact and ordered Langbehn's arrest.

All this time the Gestapo were maintaining a discreet surveillance of Goerdeler, Popitz and other figures in the Resistance. In January an entire provincial network of conspirators, the Kreisauer Circle, suffered detection and arrest, but the chief bomb-plotter Colonel Stauffenberg remained undetected because his post at the headquarters of the Replacement Army afforded a wide degree of immunity from police control.

After Stauffenberg's bomb had failed to kill Hitler on 20 July 1944 Himmler's terror machine went into top gear. All the chief conspirators were speedily arrested and sentenced to death by the notorious 'People's Court' – but the speed of the apprehension and the judicial process was in marked contrast to the tardy way in which some of the sentences were carried out. Goerdeler owed the repeated deferment of his execution to none other than Himmler himself. After first making the condemned man write out a detailed account of his peace plan, Himmler actually visited Goerdeler in his cell, where he asked him to act as an intermediary between Churchill and himself. Goerdeler indicated his agreement and asked to be allowed to travel to Sweden in furtherance of the plan, but at this point Himmler, probably thinking the Swedish trip too risky, altered course yet again and ordered Goerdeler's execution (February 1945).

Other SS dignitaries showed similar tergiversation on the eve of defeat. Dr Stuckart, the *Staatssekretar* at the Ministry of the Interior and contender for the succession to Heydrich, let a senior ministry official influence him into rephrasing and thereby virtually nullifying a directive extending the Final Solution to Jews living in mixed marriages and the offspring of all such marriages (the so-called *Mischlinge*).

The implementation of the Final Solution itself was being modified. A meeting between Himmler and the Swiss President Musi (on Austrian soil in October 1944) resulted in the saving of some thousand 'privileged' Jews for a payment of five million Swiss francs raised by Jewish organizations. (Eichmann had previously suggested similar deals to Hungarian Jewish communal leaders, but these had come to nothing.)

In October, too, Himmler ordered the blowing up of the crematoria at Auschwitz, which the Red Army was to reach three months later. This necessitated changing the nature of the deputations from Budapest: instead of being shipped off for gassing, Hungary's remaining Jews were to be force-marched to labour camps in the Reich.

The extermination programme was declared to be at an end and KZ commandants instructed accordingly. But this in no way improved the situation of camp inmates, since in order to remove tell-tale evidence Himmler had ordered the evacuation of all concentration camps in the path of the advancing Allied armies. At the same time he instructed the guards to shoot all prisoners who dropped behind; thus fully half a year after the crematoria had stopped belching smoke some approach roads into Germany were littered with corpses in zebra-striped rags.

Himmler's contradictory treatment of the Jews reflected his generally schizophrenic thinking in the last few months of the war. While one part of his mind continued to revolve around the taboo idea of approaches to the West (via such intermediaries as the Swedish consul at Budapest, Paul Wallenberg), Himmler applied all his remaining mental faculties to the prosecution of the war.

In this he showed distinct mediocrity, so that in March 1945 he was, on Guderian's urgent insistence, relieved of the command of the Army Group, Upper Rhine. The same month saw an additional erosion of the military reputation of the SS. The collapse of Sepp Dietrich's Sixth Panzer Army on the Hungarian front so enraged Hitler that he had the sleeve-bands with the names of the Sixth's constituent SS divisions – 'Das Reich', 'Adolf Hitler', 'Hohenstauffen' – ceremonially torn off the soldiers' uniforms.

Hitler's treatment of those whose 'honour meant loyalty' was soon to be reciprocated. Obergruppenführer Felix Steiner, who somewhat contentiously suggested to the Belgian SS leader Leon Degrelle that the British and Americans be greeted with banners inscribed 'Here is the anti-Soviet front', marked Hitler's fifty-sixth birthday (20 April 1945) by disobeying a directive of the Führer's to raise the siege of Berlin which would have entailed committing his 10,000-strong force to an attack on 100,000 Russians.

Yet at the same date 650 of Degrelle's Belgian Waffen SS men continued to fight the Russian crossing of the Oder until only thirty-five of their number were left alive. In fact all along the shrinking fronts SS units were still fighting doggedly – as well as executing would-be capitulators to ensure that directives for last-ditch resistance emanating from the marooned capital would be obeyed.

Now, as the Russian armies closed in on Berlin, Himmler, who saw himself as legitimate successor to the almost defunct Führer, moved towards treasonable negotiation with the enemies Germany had been fighting in her two separate, yet overlapping wars – the Jews and the Allies.

Because the Reich's Jewish War had been an encounter between total aggression and utter defencelessness without parallel in history, Himmler's parleying, though politically irrelevant, had an air of black comedy. Twenty-four hours after he had taken his final leave of Hitler and the latter's companions, who were busy celebrating the Führer's birthday in the bunker, Himmler met Norbert Masur of the World Jewish Congress at Hartzwalde in as yet unoccupied North Germany.

Masur was the first Jew Himmler had met in twelve years as an individual and not as an undifferentiated specimen of a genus doomed to extinction. Himmler opened the Hartzwalde meeting (prepared by Schellenberg and Kersten) by insisting that his emigration policy could have benefited the Jews, and blaming its failure on the obstruction of other countries. He even tried to argue that concentration camps were really retraining centres. Masur ignored this gibberish and asked that all

Jews in Nazi camps should be released and the evacuation death marches discontinued; but Himmler, still torn between fear of discovery by Hitler and the desire for an alibi for the West, would concede nothing beyond an already mooted transfer of one thousand Jewish women from Ravensbruck KZ to Sweden.

Three days later Himmler met his go-between with the West, the Swedish Count Bernadotte, at Lübeck. It was during this encounter that Himmler, who still considered himself German commander-in-chief, finally brought himself, at Schellenberg's prompting, to offer capitulation to the Western Powers, but not to the Russians. Bernadotte, who doubted the feasibility of this, asked the Reichsführer what he would do in the event of his offer being rejected. Himmler replied, 'Then I shall take command of the Eastern Front and be killed in battle.'

This statement was pure hyperbole – partly because in the short run Hitler, who heard of the Lübeck surrender offer through a BBC broadcast monitored in the bunker, posed a greater threat to Himmler's life than the Red Army. Immediately upon receiving the news Hitler had screamed out an order for Himmler's arrest and had gone on to vent his murderous rage by shooting the nearest SS man to hand, his 'brother-in-law' and liaison officer with Himmler, Hermann Fegelein.

The courier entrusted with the order for Himmler's arrest, Air Marshal von Greim (the last man to flee the besieged bunker by 'plane) caught up with the 'traitor' at the Baltic coast headquarters of Admiral Doenitz, Commander-in-Chief of the Northern Armies, but knew better than to press the matter. Doenitz remained unaware of Himmler's treachery and in fact – since news of Hitler's death was expected at any hour – looked upon the SS leader as virtually his Führer. In the event it was Doenitz himself on whom Hitler bestowed the succession in the political testament drawn up before his joint suicide with Eva Braun (30 April 1945). The sovereign period of office of the Doenitz government, from which Himmler – to his intense chagrin – found himself excluded, extended from May Day 1945 to VE Day, 8 May.

On this day Himmler shaved off his moustache and reduced his 150-strong retinue, which included Obergruppenführer Ohlendorf and von Woyrsch, to as many as could be transported in four cars. On 10 May the four cars set off in a south-westerly direction, but had to be abandoned on the right bank of the Elbe; the SS fugitives were ferried across the river by a fisherman.

Himmler, further disguised by an eye-patch, carried identity papers made out in the name of Heinrich Hitzinger (who had been executed after a 'People's Court' trial). On 23 May he was arrested at a British checkpoint and taken to 031 Interrogation Camp, where he was recognized and placed under armed guard. Later that evening an army doctor, convinced that the prisoner was concealing poison on his body, inspected Himmler's anus, hair and ears and finally order him to open his mouth. As the doctor was about to insert two fingers in his mouth Himmler suddenly bit down hard – thereby crushing a phial of poison between his teeth. Emetics and stomach pumps proved of no avail, and within minutes he was dead.

Two days later (25 May 1945) Himmler's corpse, wrapped in army blankets and camouflage netting, was interred at an unmarked spot near Lüneburg. In peacetime Sergeant-Major Edwin Austin, who performed this last office for the Reichsführer, had been a dustman.

Postscript:

Nuremberg and After

THUS HAD THE REICHSFUHRER FOLLOWED FUHRER AND REICH into limbo – into a sphere of history beyond myth or the involvement of posterity. Himmler had vanished; but what of his surviving followers – who were, incidentally, no less easily identifiable (through the bloodgroup number tattooed on their arms)?

Mowing down war-weary fellow-Germans in the process, they had fought to the last – or almost to the last. On the day of Hitler's suicide Gruppenführer Mohnke, whose *Leibstandarte* fanatics had been dragging wounded soldiers and schoolboys out of cellars and hanging them as a warning to the faint-hearted, tried to make his own escape and failed. Mohnke's case was far from unique. In this sort of conduct the upper echelons of the *Schutzstaffeln* were yet again – only this time unconsciously – aping their Reichsführer.

Had he not decreed a fight to the finish while himself engaged in surrender talks? Had he not – by the standard he had himself proclaimed – been guilty of even graver dereliction of duty when, instead of dying in battle or defiantly justifying his record before the victors' court, he had scurried away and died like a cornered rat?

The Neo-Nazi author Erich Kern* wrote in the aftermath of defeat:

'An SS officer and bearer of the Knight's Cross hanged himself in the camp latrine, leaving a note that declared he could no longer live since his Reichsführer had betrayed him. He who had denied SS suicides military burial swallowed cyanide instead of accepting responsibility and saving a hundred poor devils who had only carried out his orders from the gallows.'

The SS veteran Kern articulated a feeling common to many; Himmler, who had created the SS myth, was also instrumental in shattering it. After their liberation, news about the camps had spread, leaving an indelible stain on men's minds everywhere, but the postwar collapse of SS morale owed more to the unmarked grave near Lüneburg than to the pyramids of matchwood skeletons at Belsen.

* Erich Kern, *Der Grosse Rausch* (Zurich 1948), p. 184.

Belsen incidentally also provided a contrasting instance of the re-
covery of SS morale. By autumn 1945 local rumours were circulating
according to which the British had deliberately fed Belsen inmates to
death – besides inflating the camp's mortality figures by inscribing
'Here Lie Five Thousand' upon mass graves containing an uncounted,
but allegedly smaller, number of corpses.

But there were also countervailing instances of contrition. Obergruppenführer Herbert Backe, the former Reich Minister of Food,
before his suicide wrote to a Buchenwald survivor, Eugen Kogon,
asking forgiveness for the starvation rations he had apportioned to
concentration camp inmates.

In the aftermath of war, however, an outraged world was more concerned with the victors' retribution than with the contrition of the
defeated. The Allies set up an International Military Tribunal at
Nuremberg which (in September 1946) designated the SS as a criminal
organization and indicted the top SS leader, Ernst Kaltenbrunner, head
of the Reich Security Main Office, as a major war criminal alongside
Göring, Ribbentrop, Sauckel, Ley, Streicher, Frick, Keitel and
others.

These instigators of Nazi aggression and persecution duly ended on
the gallows – preceded by some of the more notorious (though low-
ranking) KZ guards, such as the SS maiden Irma Grese who had
amassed a collection of lamp-shades made of camp–inmates' skin.

1947–8 saw the *Einsatzgruppen* officers' trial at Nuremberg – as well
as the arraignment of the SS Economic Administration and of 'Death
Doctors' charged with KZ medical experiments. The intensification of
the Cold War at this time – the Berlin Blockade, the Communist coup
in Czechoslovakia, the Korean War – hereafter prompted the Allies to
temper justice with a degree of mercy conducive to the integration of
Germany into the Western camp, and this led to widespread
commutation of death penalties and drastic reductions of jail sentences.

The Allies' judicial appeal machinery became clogged with petitions
for clemency; when the US High Commissioner John MacCloy in July
1951 finally dismissed appeals by seven SS officials sentenced to death
in the 1947–8 trials, many Germans charged him with having played a
sadistic three-year game of cat-and-mouse.

The fate of the 'Landsberg Seven' (so-named after their place of
imprisonment) deeply stirred public opinion; a protest petition
attracted hundreds of thousands of signatures.

* Göring actually cheated the hangman by taking poison.

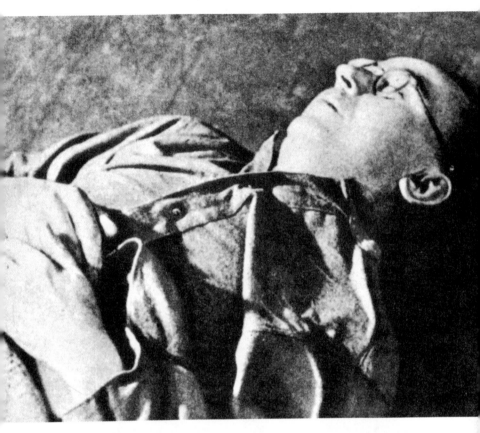

Himmler lies dead after swallowing cyanide (23 May 1945). His suicide, after a vain attempt to hide his identity, was the final blow to SS morale

The Nuremberg Trials: Ernst Kaltenbrunner, chief SS war criminal. Executed in 1946

The Nuremberg Trials: Einsatzgruppe commanders, who organised the atrocities behind the Eastern front. Otto Ohlendorf's (front row, left) appeal against his death sentence was not finally turned down until 1951

The Nuremberg Trials: Oswald
Pohl, head of the SS economic
administration, hears the
announcement of his death
sentence. (3 November 1947)

The SS rune – symbol of tyranny
to the postwar generation. Protest
at the Russian invasion of
Czechoslovakia 1968

German townscape (Aachen), 1945

At the centre of this *cause célèbre* were Oswald Pohl and Otto Ohlendorf. Both men had given an extraordinary performance in the dock. The Jew-killer Pohl compared his trial to the notorious Dreyfus case – in which a Jew had been framed by anti-Semites – and described himself as a scapegoat for Obergruppenführer Wolff and other SS dignitaries still at liberty.

Ohlendorf's conduct had been even more bizarre. While awaiting trial on a charge of ninety thousand murders this trained economist pondered the workings of imperfect competition in the Nazi economy and berated his fellow-prisoner, ex-Arms Minister Albert Speer, for having favoured large firms against artisan enterprises in the award of government contracts. Cross-examined about his rationalization of gypsy executions as 'counter-espionage measures', Ohlendorf quoted the eighteenth-century dramatist Schiller on the role of gypsy spies in the Thirty Years' War.

When asked why the tally of *Einsatzgruppe* D – ninety thousand victims – was so much lower than that of the other units, Ohlendorf replied: 'I considered it beneath me to file returns which did not correspond to the truth!'

At the time of the Landsberg controversy some eminent Waffen SS veterans – such as Paul Hausser – launched a campaign to have their old force exempted from the International Military Tribunal's blanket designation of the SS as a criminal organization. Their campaign succeeded to a remarkable extent: Chancellor Adenauer, echoed by the Social Democrat leader Ollenhauer, attested the same soldierly qualities of courage and decency to the Waffen SS as to the Wehrmacht, and furthermore brought some SS personnel within the scope of the Bonn Government's Clause 131 (which gave Nazi civil servants pensionable status in the Federal Republic).

Even though 'Clause 131 pensioners' included – at least temporarily – the first Gestapo chief Rudolf Diels, the euthanasia expert Dr Clauberg, and the widows of Heydrich and Waffen SS General Turner – who had made Serbia *judenrein* – Bonn's solicitude for the welfare and respect of SS veterans did not turn out to have been entirely misplaced.*

---

* One alternative open to those charged with liquidating the heritage of the Third Reich was a massive onslaught on all culpable institutions and individuals. The 'pragmatist' Adenauer chose the other: he proselytized the large residue of unindictable Nazis left in the Federal Republic by concessions and by emphasizing the danger of the living Stalin – or Khrushchev – rather than that of the dead Hitler.

Many of West Germany's surviving 300,000 SS soldiers had grouped themselves together in the *Hilfsgemeinschaft auf Gegenseitigkeit* (HIAG, or Mutual Help Association), a potentially dangerous veterans' organization disingenuously camouflaged as a service for tracing missing *Kameraden*.

If HIAG slowly and reluctantly veered away from outright rejection of the Bonn state towards sullen co-existence with it, the credit was due – next to Chancellor Adenauer – to the war-hero-criminal Panzer Meyer. The famous SS tank commander, who had been sentenced for the Ancienne Abbaye massacre (see p. 72) and subsequently reprieved, denounced *Kameraden* who still dwelt in the past of nationalist dreams. He went on to describe the Federal Republic as 'our state' in which HIAG members could live with their wives and children.

Some SS men took acceptance of the new state to the extent of participating in its democratic processes at a variety of levels. Ex-Sturmführer Waldemar Kraft served as Minister without Portfolio in the Adenauer cabinet, ex-Gruppenführer Reinefarth, commander of SS police units in the Warsaw Rising, was a member of the Schleswig-Holstein *Land* parliament and ex-Hauptsturmführer Otto Hunsche (Eichmann's aide in Hungary) sat on a rural district council in Hesse.

Hunsche served in local government under an assumed name – a device also used by SS entrants into higher echelons of government service. Forged papers, and highly placed friends, eased Professor Heyde, ex-euthanasia expert and medical officer at Dachau, into a key post in Schleswig-Holstein's medical service, where he actually adjudicated on the pension claims of disabled concentration camp survivors.

Other – non-medical – SS *Doktoren* entered the private sector under their own names; the goodwill of certain Ruhr industrialists enabled ex-Obergruppenführer Werner Best (Reich Plenipotentiary in Occupied Denmark) and ex-Brigadeführer Franz Six (would-be SD Plenipotentiary in Occupied Britain) to participate in the German economic miracle at middle-management level.

Reintegration into postwar life took many forms. Prior to their respective arrests in the 1960s ex-SS *Sonderkommando* officer Friedrich Meyer trained police cadets at a *Polizeischule* near Münster and ex-Sturmbannführer Helmut Bischoff (who used to punish recalcitrant slave workers in a Harz Mountain underground rocket plant by personally stringing them up) worked in the tracing service of the Red Cross.

In this climate of apparent amnesia – only apparent, because the mills of justice continued to grind slowly – some SS veterans were overcome with nostalgia. Former Obergruppenführer Wolff serialized his reminiscences in an illustrated magazine and thus unwittingly provided pointers to previously undocumented wartime atrocities; this bizarre example of 'publish and be damned' earned Wolff a fifteen year sentence.

Hotel porter Kurt Bolender's nostalgia assumed a more private form. When arrested the former assistant Lagerführer at Sobibor death camp was found to have kept the metal clasp of his horsewhip (engraved with his initials) as a memento for twenty years. Soon after, Bolender killed himself while awaiting trial at Hagen, Westphalia. A Gallup-poll taken at Hagen near the end of this trial established that the word Sobibor carried no association for nine out of ten townspeople; some thought it the name of a new detergent.

Public indifference, bureaucratic sclerosis and a dearth of surviving witnesses all combined to enfeeble the due processes of Federal law concerning war crimes. Thus the largest single murder operation of the Third Reich – that of the *Einsatzgruppen* – escaped the comprehensive attention of the judicial authorities until 1958 and might have remained unexpiated *sine die* but for the initiative of one resolute policeman. The ex-police chief of Memel, Bernhard Fischer-Schweder, filed a suit against the Federal authorities for refusing him re-employment in the police force – thereby triggering off inquiries which revealed his own part, as an SS Oberführer, in *Einsatz* massacres of Lithuanian Jews and initiating a series of *Einsatzgruppen* trials which lasted until the 1960s.

These trials helped to clarify a crucial point in all post-war controversies about the *Schutzstaffeln*: did SS men have to kill on pain of being killed themselves? Controverting the standard defence argument of indicted war criminals former Brigadeführer Six declared that *Einsatzgruppe* service could be avoided by volunteering for front-line (or other) service, and ex-Oberscharführer Matthias Graf testified that refusal of an *Einsatzgruppe* commission cost him no more than 'social disgrace' and short-term imprisonment.

The most publicized German war crimes investigation was the mammoth Auschwitz trial held at Frankfurt in 1964–5, some of the twenty-three accused bearing names that carried intimations of immortality. All had readjusted to civilian existence with remarkable facility: Oswald Kaduk as a male nurse whose Berlin patients had nicknamed him

'Papa Kaduk', and Dr Viktor Capesius (the self-styled 'Satan incarnate' of Auschwitz) as a wealthy and publicly esteemed pharmacist at Goeppingen. According to their testimony none of the accused had any inkling of 'what Auschwitz was for'; with one exception they all showed open contempt for the court.

The trials continue (though most Germans would like to see them end) – and so does the controversy about the role of the SS. Paul Hausser, the elder statesman of HIAG has of late (1966) published the self-explanatory *Soldaten wie andere auch, Der Weg der Waffen SS* – (*Soldiers like the others – the path of the Waffen SS*); in earlier books Hausser acclaimed the soldierly virtues of Oskar Dirlewanger (an executed war criminal) and Gottlob Berger (serving twenty-five years for wartime murder of Jews) – and has described the Waffen SS as an early forerunner of NATO.

Adolf von Thadden and his co-founders of the NPD held the well-publicized inaugural meeting of their Party at the graveside of the Landsberg Seven – on the assumption that the 'blood of its martyrs will fructify the Church'. At the Federal elections of 1969 the National Democrats polled 4.3 per cent of the votes cast.

Elsewhere in the world there is unanimity about the role of the *Schutzstaffeln*. The initials SS are likely to remain symbols of abominable tyranny for generations to come. In Spring 1968 French youths born long after Oradour screamed them at the French special riot police – a few months later, on the other side of Europe, enraged Czechs born long after Lidice scrawled 'U ϟϟR' on Soviet tanks.

The SS is a never-to-be-forgotten automaton that desolated Europe and left the world a poorer and darker place. Jewish legend tells of the Golem, a clay monster which a wonder-rabbi animated by placing the letter 'CHAI' (Hebrew for 'life') in its mouth.

The SS was no monster of clay but of flesh and blood. The letters animating it were 'TOD' (German for 'death'). But Hitler, though a worker of wonders, was no priest. His priestly power was derived from Nietzsche, who had written in *Thus Spake Zarathustra*: 'Ye say a good cause will hallow even war? I say unto you a good war halloweth every cause.'

Notes on Further Reading

Hans Buchheim, *The Third Reich*, London 1961
Alan Bullock, *Hitler, A Study in Tyranny*, London 1952
Edward Crankshaw, *Gestapo – Instrument of Tyranny*, London 1965
Richard Grunberger, *Germany – 1918–1945*, London 1964
Gideon Hausner, *Justice in Jerusalem*, London 1967
Eugen Kogon, *The Theory and Practice of Hell*, London 1950
H. Krausnick, H. Buchheim, M. Broszat and H. A. Jacobsen, *Anatomy of the SS State*, London 1969
R. Manvell and H. Fraenkel, *Himmler*, London 1965
Bernard Naumann, *Auschwitz*, London 1966
Gerald Reitlinger, *The Final Solution*, London 1953
Gerald Reitlinger, *The SS – Alibi of a Nation*, London 1956
Hans Rothfels, *The German Opposition to Hitler*, London 1960
William Shirer, *The Rise and Fall of the Third Reich*, London 1960
J. Wheller-Bennett, *The Nemesis of Power*, London 1952

Glossary

HIAG   Mutual Help Association for SS soldiers
KZ   Concentration-Camp
OKW   Supreme Command of the Armed Forces
RSHA   Reich Security Main Office
RUSHA   Race and Settlement Main Office
SA   Storm Troopers
SD   SS Intelligence Service
WVHA   Economic Administration Main Office
Abwehr   Military Intelligence
Ahnenerbe   SS foundation for research into Ancestral Heritage
Asoziale   Anti-social (i.e. criminal or work-shy) concentration camp
   inmates
Bildungsbürgertum   Middle class by virtue of education (as distinct
   from wealth)
Braunes Haus   Nazi Party headquarters in Munich
Eindeutschung   Germanization, i.e. turning foreign nationals into
   Germans
Einsatzgruppe   Operational group carrying out liquidations in
   occupied territory
Frauenlager   Concentration camp for women
Freikorps   Right-wing para-military bands active after 1918
Gauleiter   Highest Nazi Party leader in a Gau, or province of the
   Third Reich
Gestapo   Secret State Police
Gleichschaltung   Co-ordination or alignment with the Nazi state
Gouvernement-Général   Nazi-occupied Poland
Innenministerium   Reich Ministry of the Interior
Iron Guard   Rumanian Fascist organization
Judenrein   Cleared of Jews
Judenreservat   A cluster of ghettoes
Kamerad   Comrade – customary form of address within formations of
   the Nazi Party.

Kleinbürger   Petty bourgeois

Kristallnacht   Crystal Night, the pogrom of 10 November 1938, so-called on account of the shattered windows of Jewish shops

Lager   Concentration (or prison) camp

Lebensborn   Fountain of Life foundation – an SS adoption and child-kidnapping organization.

Leibstandarte   Hitler's bodyguard

Mischling   Person of mixed German-Jewish parentage

Ostindustrie Ges.m.b.H.   Eastern Industry Ltd

Protektorat   Nazi-occupied Bohemia and Moravia

Putsch   Attempted *coup d'état*

Reichstag   German Parliament

Reichswehr   German Army; in 1935 its name was changed to Wehrmacht

Reiter SS   Mounted SS

Schutzstaffeln   Protective Squads

Spartacists   Forerunners of the German Communist Party

'*Das Schwarze Korps*'   Official weekly of the SS

Sonderkommando   Special SS task force

Stosstruppe   Shock troops

Sturmabteilung   Stormtroopers

Totenkopf   Death's Head

Verfügungstruppe   Militarized formations of SS, renamed Waffen-SS in the winter of 1939–40

Volksdeutsche   Germans living outside the Reich

Volksgruppe   The body of Volksdeutsche within one specific country

Volksgemeinschaft   The Folk community – the Nazi-projected image of a harmonious society

Waffen SS   *see* Verfügungstruppe

Wehrkreis   A Military District

Wehrmacht   *see* Reichswehr

Weimar Republic The German democratic state constituted in 1919 and destroyed by the Nazis in 1933

Table of Ranks

SS	GERMAN ARMY	BRITISH ARMY
Reichsführer	Generalfeldmarschall	Field Marshal
Obergruppenführer	General	General
Gruppenführer	Generalleutnant	Lieutenant-General
Brigadeführer	Generalmajor	Major-General
Oberführer	Oberst	Brigadier
Standartenführer	Oberst	Colonel
Obersturmbannführer	Oberstleutnant	Lieutenant-Colonel
Sturmbannführer	Major	Major
Hauptsturmführer	Hauptmann	Captain
Obersturmführer	Oberleutnant	Lieutenant
Untersturmführer	Leutnant	Second Lieutenant
Sturmscharführer	Stabsfeldwebel	Regimental Sergeant-Major
Hauptscharführer	Oberfeldwebel	Sergeant-Major
Oberscharführer	Feldwebel	Quartermaster-Sergeant
Scharführer	Unterfeldwebel	Staff Sergeant
Unterscharführer	Unteroffizier	Sergeant
Rottenführer	Gefreiter	Corporal
Sturmann	Oberschütze	Lance-Corporal
SS-Mann	Schütze	Private

Index